Graeme Croser is an award-winning sports writer with close to 25 years' experience in the regional and national press covering domestic, European and international action. The Napier University journalism graduate served with the *Edinburgh Evening News* before spending 19 years with the *Scottish Mail on Sunday*. He is a past winner of the Jim Rodger Memorial Award, which recognises the work of Scotland's best young sports writers.

Hey Jude

The Rise and Rise of Jude Bellingham

Graeme Croser

First published in 2024 by
Arena Sport, an imprint of
Birlinn Limited
West Newington House
10 Newington Road
Edinburgh
EH9 1QS
www.arenasportbooks.co.uk

ISBN 978 1 913759 21 6

British Library Cataloguing-in-Publication Data
A catalogue record for this book is available from the British Library

Typeset by Initial Typesetting Services, Edinburgh

Papers used by Birlinn are from well-managed forests
and other responsible sources

Printed and bound by Clays Ltd, Elcograf S.p.A.

For Caleb, Noah and Freya

CONTENTS

ACKNOWLEDGEMENTS

It's one thing to file a newspaper article in the teeth of a tight deadline, quite another to piece together an entire book at short order.

Special thanks to Davide Ancelotti, who took time out from his Champions League Final preparations to meet me in Madrid. Paul Lambert, Michael Beale, Lukas Jutkiewicz, Pep Clotet, Ramón Calderón, Aidy Boothroyd, Darren Burgess, Joe Chapman, Oliver Müller and Guillem Balagué were also generous with their time and insight.

Big mentions to Graham Hunter, a whirlwind of ideas and energy, and the ever-perceptive Jonathan Northcroft, who both went above and beyond in helping me bring this project to life. I should also apologise to Graham for fluffing the Bowie backing vocals in Berlin.

I'm grateful to Tam Courts, Derek McInnes and Alan Burrows for opening doors while Paul Smith at Birlinn has been a calm and gently encouraging editor, a revelation after some trying professional times.

Thanks to Mum, Dad, Angela, Joanne and Gerard for all their support, likewise Tommy Guthrie, Steven Galbraith, Iain Park, Francesca di Mambro, Alan Pattullo, Gordon

Waddell, Mark Wilson, Graeme Bryce, David Murrie, Emma Monaghan, Frank and Lynn McWilliams, Ramsay Laing, Fraser Mackie, Guy Woodford, Scott McDermott, Danny Stewart, Michael Grant, John Greechan, Hugh MacDonald, Andrew Simmons, Lorne Gardner, Martin Keegan, Derek Rae, Mark Guidi and Ewan Murray.

I'd like to pay tribute to Goodbye Mr Mackenzie for a priceless education in the discipline of storytelling.

And lastly, thanks to Jude Bellingham for providing such compelling subject matter.

Pleasingly, it looks like we're just getting started.

Graeme Croser
September 2024

Chapter 1

LOS BLANCOS, LA VIDA

THANK you for coming and welcome home. The words of Florentino Pérez to Jude Bellingham on the occasion of his presentation as a Real Madrid player to the world's media. A charismatic and authoritative club president and father of the Galacticos project, Pérez has never been a man to knowingly underplay his hand, but this truly was a statement signing, one to underscore the club's status as *the* dream destination for the most talented young players on the planet.

Still two weeks short of his 20th birthday, Bellingham arrived from Borussia Dortmund in June 2023 as the Bundesliga player of the year and an established England international who had starred at the World Cup six months previously. The deal, for an initial outlay of £88.5 million, ranked as the club's second most expensive signing of all time. Dressed in a sharp black suit and tie, the teenager followed Pérez on to the podium and spoke with the clarity and assurance of someone a decade older: 'Thank you everyone for joining me on the proudest day of my life. The day where I joined the greatest football club in the history of the game.'

Madrid's imperiousness had come under threat from the petro dollars funnelled into clubs such as Manchester City and Paris Saint-Germain from the oil-rich Middle East. In common with the rest of the Premier League elite, City had been keen to secure Bellingham since his breakthrough year at Birmingham City when, aged just 16, he'd thrived during a full season in England's punishing second tier. When he was sold by his home-town club at the end of that season, he could easily have joined Manchester United, Chelsea or Arsenal. Instead, he'd chosen the route less ordinary and moved to Germany and Borussia Dortmund, a brave transfer that came with added complications during the midst of the Covid pandemic.

Bellingham flourished in the Bundesliga and, by his second year, was one of the team's leaders and a seasoned Champions League performer. After a third he was an England regular and ripe for another move and, despite the best efforts of Liverpool and City in particular, he would shun a move home in favour of the ultimate destination: Madrid.

It takes a special type of player, a certain personality, to shine with Los Blancos. Pérez and his key members of staff – a streamlined group featuring general manager José Ángel Sánchez, chief scout Juni Calafat and the coach Carlo Ancelotti – clearly believed that Bellingham had the personality to match his talent. As much as the capture of Bellingham was an expensive feather in the Madrid cap, it wasn't a coup to capture the imagination of the masses in the way, say, David Beckham or Cristiano Ronaldo's arrivals did at the height of the Galacticos era in the noughties.

The previous season had been chastening, with a league title ceded too easily to Barcelona and the European crown toppled from their heads thanks to a drubbing from City that bordered on humiliation. With the stadium still a partial building site due to ongoing renovations, this was deemed no time and no stage for grandstanding. Accordingly, there was to be no public Santiago Bernabéu unveiling for Jude à la Ronaldo or indeed Kylian Mbappé, who'd join from PSG to much fanfare a year later. And so Jude, flanked by his mother Denise, father Mark and brother Jobe, was treated to a cosier introduction strictly by invitation only, at Madrid City, the training complex housed at the Valdebebas development to the east of the city.

'Jude wasn't an automatic Galactico, he wasn't Mbappé,' reasons Spanish journalist Guillem Balague. 'He came to Real Madrid as the best player in the Bundesliga and as maybe one of the best youngsters around, but not with the kind of reputation that will open the Santiago Bernabéu. Madrid are very aware of their image and what works at that level and what doesn't.'

At this club, in front of an infamously tough crowd, it was absurdly premature to dream of a stadium of Madridistas singing the words to 'Hey Jude' in perfect harmony. Such adulation would take years, not to mention significant good fortune, to earn. Wouldn't it . . . ?

*

The Santiago Bernabéu is one of world football's great cathedrals. After a lengthy, extensive and intricate facelift it can now lay a strong claim to be the premier stadium on the planet. This latest refurbishment has taken nearly five years and €800 million and the specifications are mind-boggling. A capacity of 84,000, with spectators accommodated on eight tiers of seating, and a 360-degree wraparound screen that hangs below a new retractable roof designed to offer protection from the weather but enhance the noise generated within the stadium. The renovation has also incorporated a new pitch storage and removal system, which allows for the playing surface to be housed and tended to on what is, essentially, a multi-tiered underground greenhouse.

The stadium, situated on the site of the club's old Chamartín home, was named with appropriate modesty after the club's then president in 1955. Situated on La Castellana, the long thoroughfare around which the city's financial district thrives, it boasts an exclusive address. Yet from the outside it is a little underwhelming. The curved steel plates on the outside reflect only the greyness of the urban surrounds. And while the shape is interesting – think a ginormous-scale version of the 'bean' sculpture in downtown Chicago – it lacks the magnetism of Anish Kapoor's reflective installation. This exterior is not dissimilar in design to Munich's Allianz Arena, but Bayern's home benefits from a location detached from the city which allows it to dominate the horizon.

Yet these are mere aesthetics. The stadium's interior is entirely impressive and is a worthy successor to the previous incarnations which served as the stage of Alfredo Di Stéfano and Ferenc Puskás, of Emilio Butragueño and Raúl, Luís Figo and Zinedine Zidane and the two uniquely gifted Ronaldos. With its raft of corporate and hospitality suites and an updated football museum, it is also a key plank of Madrid's strategy to drive enough revenue to keep the club at the peak of the game.

Few men understand the fabric and the personality of the club better than its 16th president, Ramón Calderón. The lawyer no longer holds a title at the club but his office is situated just a few blocks away from the stadium in downtown Madrid. A regular media contributor, he remains a passionate and vocal supporter of the club, and sometimes a critic. On approach, his premises seem modest, but once through the thick wooden door and up a short flight of stairs, the office interior opens out just as one might imagine. There are rows of books on the shelves, a substantial writing desk and a separate conference table detached in a window area with a view. Raymond Burr could quite happily have got into character in this place.

'There are many reasons why Real Madrid is unique,' he begins. 'This is a special club because it is not a company. It is a non-profit association so that means you need to rely on your own resources in order to be sustainable and be able to compete with teams owned by oligarchs, by states and big companies. You are just a non-profit association with 90,000 members who only pay €150 a year which is only 2 or 3 per cent of the budget, nothing, so we have to be able to organise properly with TV, marketing and ticketing. Seventy-five per cent of the people living in Madrid – including me – weren't born in the city. So we are not linked to the club by regional or local feeling like in Manchester, Liverpool or Barcelona. We are linked with the success. People here are very demanding. Go to the stadium and you can feel that.'

Despite the competition from City, PSG and the traditional rivals such as Bayern Munich, Juventus, Manchester United and of course Barcelona, Madrid topped Deloitte's Football Money League in 2024. Announced on the basis of a relatively fallow season to the summer of 2023, the figures depict revenue of £723 million, a sum that is only likely to increase as the full power of the stadium is rolled out. Coupled with a new, more considered transfer strategy less focused on names and more with a view on the path stretching ahead in the distance, Madrid appear future-proofed.

Ancelotti has remarked that Pérez, now in his late seventies, has grown tired of the constant turbulence that he actively fomented in his younger years, constantly churning his way through a revolving cast of coaches and big-name signings. Yet this would appear to be a relatively recent awakening. After returning to the club for a second spell as president in 2009, he continued the Galacticos project by landing the likes of Gareth Bale (£85 million, 2013) and James Rodríguez (£63 million, 2014).

Despite a strong maiden season in Spain following his move from Monaco, Rodríguez never fully delivered on the promise he showed during a spectacular outing for Colombia during the 2014 World Cup and was even sent out on loan to Bayern Munich for two years to stem the flow of wasted wages. A spectacular success for two-thirds of his spell in Spain, Bale won 15 trophies and his outrageous overhead kick in the 2018 Champions League final was a moment to rival Zidane at Hampden for sheer magnificence on the biggest stage. But his final three years at the club were a tale of recrimination and atrophy as the Welshman sat out his contract and eventually departed for nothing. The story of Eden Hazard was a throwback to a more reckless time, from the Belgian's record £97 million transfer from Chelsea through to the termination of his contract in 2023. Beset by problems, he subsequently retired from football aged 32.

And yet amid all the largesse, Madrid could also be ruthless. Cristiano Ronaldo was the undisputed king of Madrid for each of his nine seasons at the club and was still scoring at a phenomenal rate during what proved to be his final season in white. His reward for rattling in 44 goals in 44 games? A transfer to Juventus that shocked many yet crucially registered a profit for a club that had almost gloried in its disregard for prudence. Similarly, the club was brutal in its treatment of its legendary captain Sergio Ramos. A product of the club's academy and a trophy magnet for club and country, Ramos was offered an opportunity to renew his contract in 2021. Perhaps he didn't believe the hierarchy when they placed a hard deadline on the offer, but when he failed to respond within the allotted time, he was cut loose. Mindful of the Bale and Rodríguez situations, Raphael Varane and Casemiro were sold to Manchester United for a premium just as their performances suggested they were entering a period of decline.

With Calafat to the fore, Madrid started to source younger players earlier in their careers. Brazilians Vinicius Jr, Rodrygo and Endrick were secured in their teens, while the French duo of Eduardo Camavinga and Aurélien Tchouaméni were also brought in at a cost, but well below their projected market ceilings. At £88.5 million, Bellingham was most expensive of all, but he too was perceived to be worth the long-term investment.

The 2023–24 season had the potential to be one of transition for the club, and therefore one in which Ancelotti could have run out of road for a second time. The main adjustment surrounded the departure of striker Karim Benzema, a reliable and prolific goalscorer who had spearheaded the team for a decade and more, delivering goals at a rate of 354 in 648 games and lifting 25 trophies, a tally matched only in Madrid history by Brazilian defender Marcelo. Rather than directly replace him, Madrid instead put faith in a longer-term transfer strategy.

The forward they really wanted, Mbappé, would not be available for another year, but was deemed worth the wait and the expense to finally lure him away from Paris in the summer of 2024. Instead, the marquee summer arrival would be a lad about to celebrate his 20th birthday. Madrid is not an easy club at which to settle. And Bellingham was only the sixth English player to give it a try.

David Beckham is the most high-profile example, but he had been preceded by Steve McManaman and, even earlier, Laurie Cunningham. Midlands football was in fashion in 1979. Just a few months after Trevor Francis became Britain's first £1 million player courtesy of his transfer between Birmingham City and Nottingham Forest, Cunningham became the first Brit to sign for Real Madrid, with a sum just short of seven figures being paid to West Brom for his services. He made a bright start, scoring twice on his debut and snaring a league and cup double in his first season. From there, injury and the restrictions on the quota of foreign players conspired to squeeze him towards the exit. Cunningham did retain an affinity for the city, returning twice to sign for Rayo Vallecano before his tragic death in a car crash in Madrid in 1989. He was just 33.

While Barcelona went through a few British players – Gary Lineker, Mark Hughes and Steve Archibald all featured in the mid to late 1980s – Madrid tended to look elsewhere until Liverpool's McManaman became available on a Bosman transfer in 1999. At 27 and seasoned as a high-level club and international player, McManaman was eager to adapt and threw himself into the lifestyle and the language, factors that helped his already proven talent flourish at his new club. By the end of his first year he was a Champions League winner, having volleyed in a goal in the 3-0 victory over Valencia in the Paris final. He'd stay four years in total, winning two La Liga titles and adding a second Champions League winner's medal courtesy of a substitute appearance in the team's victory over Bayer Leverkusen in Glasgow in 2002, a match best remembered for Zinedine Zidane's majestic goal.

McManaman's departure coincided with the arrival of David Beckham who eventually found a way to coexist with a star-studded and sceptical dressing room cast, but subsequent recruits fared less well. Michael Owen arrived a year later with a big reputation and a Ballon d'Or trophy already on his CV, yet at just 24, his best, explosive years were already behind him. Jonathan Woodgate, a centre-back who'd excelled firstly at Leeds and then Newcastle, arrived in the same window and was plagued with injuries.

'Michael Owen didn't particularly engage in the culture,' says Spanish-based journalist Graham Hunter. 'Culturally, if you are out of step, the bus can leave you behind really quickly. He also needed and wanted a particular way of playing which, at that stage, Madrid weren't well equipped to provide. Owen was a smart student of his art. He understood the science but he needed a certain type of service. He'd been great coming through at Liverpool, then for England which startled the world. But by the time he came to Madrid, the muscles had rusted a little bit.

'Jonathan Woodgate should have been better equipped because his game was not predicated on pace and the ability to finish. His art was letting the play come on to him and he should have had directly transferable skills. One thing after another went against him. He was liked. He adapted in a way that Michael Owen didn't. Michael's aptitude for learning Spanish or living the Spanish life were not right for thriving, but Woodgate was popular and he could have thrived. There are a myriad of ways things can go wrong. A lack of preparation, a misapprehension that Real Madrid is just another continental club, bad luck, injuries or having a teammate who is a direct enemy because they resent you. Any of those things can prevent you doing well at Madrid. But Jude was perfectly equipped mentally and physically. That winner's attitude is the number one thing that Real Madrid recognise.'

And yet even the most heralded of players, men who have written their way into Madrid folklore, can struggle to cope with the weight of playing for a club that demands to win and to do so in style. The signing of Cristiano Ronaldo is regarded as the high point of Calderón's presidency. He had to fight long and hard to prise the Portuguese forward from United's grips and even had to resist Ferguson's preferred plan to sell him to Barcelona. The capture of a supreme attacker in his prime ought to have been cause for instant celebration and, at least for the duration of his packed presentation at the stadium, it was. But when the football started, the crowd was not slow in expressing its demands – and disapproval that he was not immediately up to scratch.

'It is very difficult to be successful here,' continues Calderón. 'Cristiano came here having won the Ballon d'Or and the Champions League and still the fans were very critical of him. Zidane signed in July and was booed in November. Some of the players I've had here couldn't really understand why people were so cold, coming from places like Manchester and so on. I remember we played Man United in 2003 and we were winning 3-2, and 6-3 on aggregate, with Ronaldo Nazário scoring all three goals. And yet the Old Trafford crowd was still there backing their team, singing and cheering. Here it is not like that. If we were three goals behind at the Bernabéu, people would be booing with their handkerchiefs, and some of them would be leaving. I think players feel that and that's why it's very difficult to be successful here.'

'I've been dealing with that club long enough to remember when they signed Ronaldo Nazário,' says Hunter, picking up the thread. 'Which was a coup, given that he was a World Cup winner and ex-Barcelona, a player at the peak of his powers. He had won the World Cup and that meant he became the Ballon d'Or winner. This was a Galactico time, when they all believed Florentino Pérez was untouchable. Madrid were on the crest of a wave and they had this world genius – he was announced on the pitch as: "Ronaldo, our Ballon d'Or winner." And the crowd whistled. They didn't boo but they began to chant "Raúl! Raúl!

Raúl!" As if to say: "We don't give two hoots who you are, what you have won, what you have done; we want Raúl to be the Ballon d'Or." That tells you a little bit about the personality of that club and how you can't always anticipate what they are going to feel and how they are going to welcome you.

'Another example would be Vinicius. When he arrived he was younger than Jude and nowhere near as formed. But they shat on him, both the media and the fans – he has custard for brains, can't finish, in the crucial moments around the goalmouth the synapses are not connected. And in the media in particular, and this is my strong opinion and I am delighted to go on the record with this, I think he was treated in a racist way. Because he was a black Brazilian, not a Spaniard. The treatment was ridiculous. I think he has been treated disgustingly.

'Those are only two examples of the context of the environment into which Jude Bellingham came. Gareth Bale's winning record – his crucial goals and trophy record – is astonishing. And yet in the latter years of his contract he was dismissed as a dosser. By the time Iker Casillas left he was kind of at war with a lot of the media and some of the fans. Falsely or accurately nailed as someone who leaked the team to friends in the media. There is a history of those who have literally rewritten Real Madrid history being ostracised or pushed out of the door and don't forget to close it behind you.

'Bellingham arrives as a 20-year-old without any Spanish to a team which has lost a genuine all-time superstar in Benzema. So those expectations and demands fell upon a 20-year-old Englishman with just two really strong seasons behind him. Dortmund is a relatively underachieving club; it's not as if he was facing a tenth of the pressure or demands he has at Madrid. And then you add in the fact you are working for a president who sacked Carlo Ancelotti first time and said: "Out of date, thank you and goodbye."

'The club as an institution is haughty. Player after player will tell you that their professional player care is exceptional. But it's not a club that wraps you in love and affection. They've given you the tools now get on with your job. It's a good life but that's because of how well you can live in Madrid and how wealthy you are. But there is really no safety net. And Jude came into a dressing room which was universally disgusted with itself having allowed a pretty debilitated Barcelona to win the league and win it well.'

From the Basque Country to Cadiz, a feeling persists throughout Spain, whether wholly justified or not, that Madrid remains the establishment club, one that was favoured by General Franco, the dictator who ruled the country for four decades from the 1930s. Calderón would not deny that there is a culture of entitlement around the club, but he sees the institution as a force for good, one that transcends domestic issues, be they political or geographical. 'Real Madrid is the club of Spain,' he states. 'Just like Juventus is the club of Italy, not the club of Turin. I think Real Madrid represents Spain very well and, for me, is one of its best ambassadors. Everywhere you go it's amazing. You say you are from Spain and the response: "Oh, Real Madrid." It's instinctive.'

For one former coach, José Mourinho, the secret of Madrid's success is much easier to define: 'It's such a simple structure. Florentino Pérez. José Ángel Sánchez. And the chief scout. And the coach. Simplicity is genius.' All four of those individuals were personally involved in the acquisition of Bellingham although ironically it's Ancelotti, his mentor and manager, who probably had the least input.

On day one, Bellingham managed to pull off the winning combination of feeling both incredibly fortunate to have landed in Spain while conveying a sense that he truly belonged. Recruited on a six-year contract that would reportedly earn him an eight-figure annual salary, he spoke persuasively of how the decision had been motivated by football and not finance.

He said: 'I don't think about money when I make these kinds of decisions. I never have and I never will. I play the game purely out of love. When I was given permission by Borussia Dortmund I spoke with Juni (Calafat) and José Ángel (Sanchez) and I loved the feeling I got from the club. I couldn't hide it. I told them more or less straight away what I felt about the club and once I made my decision I wanted it to happen quickly. It wasn't a case of the other teams are bad or they weren't good, it's just that for me, Madrid is the greatest. It was a bit of a surprise when my dad sat me down and said, "You've had a bit of interest from Real Madrid," 12, 15 months ago maybe. It was goosebumps and my heart was close to stopping because it's just something you don't expect growing up. So when it manifests itself it's just such an amazing feeling.'

Humbled perhaps, but definitely not shy. Jude's decision to take Madrid's No. 5 jersey was laced with symbolism. He'd made no secret of his admiration for Zinedine Zidane, and some observers, including his former coach at Dortmund René Marić, had even compared him directly to the Frenchman, a World Cup winner and an immediately recognisable symbol of the Galacticos era.

Traditionally the preserve of hard-nosed centre-backs, the No. 5 had arrived on Zidane's back at a time when Madrid's lavish signing policy meant the best ball technicians on the planet were also forced to get creative in their handling of numbers. In 2001, when Pérez struck the deal to land Zidane from Juventus, he was unable to hand the playmaker his trademark No. 10 shirt. That's because the arrival of Luís Figo, in a politically incendiary transfer from Barcelona a year earlier, had included an accommodation for the Portuguese star's second favourite number. Figo would have preferred the No. 7 but that jersey was already in the possession of Raúl, a home-grown totem of the club's academy and a poster boy for the Spanish national team.

When David Beckham later arrived from Manchester United in 2003 he too deferred to Raúl, declaring him 'the king of Real Madrid'. And with Figo still holding the No. 10 he instead settled on the No. 23, citing Michael Jordan as an inspiration. Jordan, the finest basketball player of all time, had also worn 23. One might wish to add some mythical quality to Jordan's choice – 23 is a prime number – yet the truth was more prosaic. As a child, Jordan imitated his older brother, who wore the number 45. When they played together in high school they could not wear the same number so Jordan decided to split it in half and round up by half a decimal point to 23.

By nothing but sheer coincidence, Bellingham started his career wearing 22, a number charged with meaning but chosen via the logic of arithmetic. The spark was provided by Mike Dodds, an academy coach during Jude's ascent through the ranks at Birmingham City. 'He challenged me,' recalled Bellingham. 'He said: "You're good at ten, good at eight and good at four, but how many midfielders, especially English midfielders, can do all three? I don't want you to play as just one when you have the attributes to do it all."'

For any tactic-heads reading, a little clarification may be required. In common coaching parlance, the deep-lying midfielder is known as the pivot, anchor, holder or, in numerical terms, 'the six'. Bellingham, and Dodds, clearly associated the role with the number four, perhaps as a consequence of the player's love and reverence for Steven Gerrard, who routinely wore four when playing for England.

Jude has always strived to be more than one thing. 'I probably prefer playing as an eight, just getting box to box,' he said earlier in his career. 'But if the manager wants me to play as a four I can do that too. I like tackling, getting stuck in, but as an eight I can dictate play too. I have a bit of an edge to me when I'm on the pitch and I like to show that when I make tackles and stuff. Being involved in every aspect of the game is better than being greedy for goals.'

The No. 22 had graced his back at Birmingham, Dortmund and also with England at the 2022 World Cup in Qatar, but now he was shedding it to happily take on the mantle of one of his idols. 'It's just a number,' he said. 'I try to wear it with my own swagger and style. I'm not trying to be Zinedine Zidane, I'm trying to be Jude Bellingham but, my God, it's not a bad person to be put in the same sentence as.'

It's this attitude, this willingness to take on the burden of expectation that gave him such a chance to make a success of playing for Madrid. Assistant coach Davide Ancelotti has worked under his father in all of Europe's big leagues. Now in his second spell at Madrid, he insists nothing compares. 'The greatness that surrounds you is different from any other club,' he explains. 'Everywhere you go is full of Madrid fans. It is incredible. Every airport we go to in every country it's incredible. So everything you do is under the lights. It's a difficult place to be. But Jude fits very well because I think he prepared to be here mentally. The communication he has, how he talks to the media and how he talks before games is very good. The expectation is incredibly high. But I don't know if it's because of Real Madrid or the opposite. If Real Madrid is so great because of the expectations that the manager has to win a title every single season. If he doesn't he is on the verge of the sack. That's unique in the world – you don't have another club like this. When you work here you know this. You know that even if you make the best season and you don't win a title you have to leave as a manager.'

The Ancelottis were about to place their trust in Jude. It's not a stretch to surmise that he repaid that faith by saving their jobs.

Chapter 2

INSTANT IMPACT

NUEVE meses de invierno y tres de infierno. Oft-repeated by Madrileños with a sigh, the saying offers a downbeat take on the climate tolerated by the citizens of the Spanish capital: nine months of winter and three months of hell. The same motto might be applied by the football fan who spends three quarters of the year venerating the superstars of Real Madrid. When the football stops they spend the sweltering summer months trying to cool their homes and calm their impatience for the new season to arrive.

The summer of 2023 was no different but there was a little extra angst in the air as supporters sought respite from the oppressive heat. Traditionally, Real Madrid like to mark their summers with at least one grandstand signing, the purchase of a world-class player who underscores the club's sense of entitlement and supremacy. In the era of the Galacticos this meant established names like Luís Figo, Zinedine Zidane and David Beckham were paraded for the cameras alongside club president Florentino Pérez.

The policy of signing the best players in the world has not changed, but the profile of those targeted has shifted. The extensive, expensive refurbishment of the Santiago

Bernabéu has been one obvious factor. When it comes to transfers, value now trumps vanity. Rather than go for the superstar who has already been over the course several times, Madrid like to invest in the brightest young talent in the aim of securing an extended return on their outlay. They are prepared to pay a premium too, confident that resale value is baked into a new signing the moment a white shirt is placed upon his shoulders.

The enhancement in football data software means clubs the world over – whether rich or comparatively poor – have access to the same statistics and, as a consequence, there are far fewer hidden gems. To maintain their place at the top of the football food chain, Madrid have switched their focus to catch the best early. Confident that the Madrid name will always be alluring to the cream of European talent, the club's chief scout Juni Calafat has also specifically targeted the South American market.

And so when the Brazilian starlet Vinicius Jr debuted for Flamengo aged 16 in 2017, Madrid were already across the situation. Within days the winger had agreed a deal to join the club in an astonishing £38.7 million transfer which would come into effect after his 18th birthday in 2018. His subsequent impact has converted that apparently wild gamble into an astute investment. Any sense that Madrid got lucky with Vinicius can be laid to rest by the fact they repeated the trick a year later with the capture of his compatriot Rodrygo. This time it was Santos, the club who fostered the great Pelé, who had felt compelled to unleash their young prodigy at 16 and two years later they were cashing in for a similar fee.

Closer to home, Madrid also had eyes on Eduardo

Camavinga as he broke through at Rennes as a 16-year-old, and captured him two years later in 2021. Aurélien Tchouaméni had to take an extra step to Monaco after emerging at Bordeaux but he still arrived at the Santiago Bernabéu as a 22-year-old with his best years ahead.

Likewise with Jude Bellingham. Established at Dortmund and a World Cup scorer with England, Bellingham was hardly an unknown quantity. Indeed his acquisition in the face of hardened Premier League interest from Manchester City and Liverpool represented a feather in the cap for Pérez, an endorsement of Madrid's continuing pre-eminence in the game.

The trouble was that he was not viewed by many, perhaps including head coach Carlo Ancelotti, as precisely what the club needed. Madrid's data harvesters had already stacked the club's midfield with young energetic talent in the previous summers, adding Camavinga and Tchouaméni to a roster already including the hard-running Uruguayan Federico Valverde and seasoned masters Toni Kroos and Luka Modrić. Where Madrid really needed a game-changing upgrade was in attack, specifically at centre-forward following Karim Benzema's surprise decision to head off for the riches of the Saudi Pro League.

At 35, Benzema might have been past his very best, but he had been a consistent and lethal finisher for Madrid for 14 years and, as recently as 2022, had won the Ballon d'Or prize to be crowned as the world's best footballer. Madrid like to plan their big buys in advance, and the thinking was that Benzema would stick around for another year and leave just at the moment his natural successor and compatriot Kylian Mbappé finally became available. Instead,

Benzema decided to grab the cash on offer at Al-Ittihad and left Madrid hanging, blindsiding Ancelotti in the process.

The loan signing of Espanyol's Joselu, who'd previously toiled for the likes of Stoke City and Newcastle, was surely not going to cut it. Many in the know have suggested Ancelotti was strongly in favour of a move for Harry Kane. Yet here Madrid were, negotiating a loan for a striker from the city of Barcelona's second club during a summer where they were ostensibly playing catch-up to their greatest rivals.

Barça had taken the La Liga title with four games to spare, and would have prevailed sooner if not for a drop-off in form in the early part of 2023. The capture of the Copa del Rey ensured it was no barren year for Madrid, but there was tangible pressure on Ancelotti going into the new season. Pérez had brought Ancelotti back to the club in 2021 as a replacement for Zidane, who himself had been brought back for a second stint in charge following an earlier exit. Madrid hire and fire at such a rate that few take it personally when the axe falls.

Historically, competency and a proven track record have counted for little when Pérez has decided it's time to order something new from the menu. The Italian's first spell featured the capture of Madrid's tenth European Cup victory, the coveted and much-celebrated 'Decima'. It mattered not a jot that this also stood as Ancelotti's third personal success in the competition as a manager following his triumphs at AC Milan; a year later he was gone with Pérez citing the huge demands at Madrid and the need for a 'new impulse' to satisfy them. Ancelotti shrugged his shoulders, took a brief sabbatical and within six months had signed a contract to replace Pep Guardiola at Bayern Munich.

It was in Munich that his son Davide, who'd first joined his backroom staff as a fitness coach at Paris Saint-Germain, was promoted to the role of assistant coach. Although Ancelotti Snr has remained resolutely independent – some might say old school – in his philosophy, Davide provides modernity, and a natural link to the younger players in the squad.

So it was when the signing of Bellingham was confirmed at Madrid. The purchase of Bellingham for a tidy sum of £88.5 million had been in the pipeline for a year and the manager was fully briefed. Still, it represented a huge outlay in a department of the squad in which reinforcements were not urgently required. Fluent in English and, at 34, young enough to relate, Davide assumed a key role in helping the new lad settle. Afforded some downtime after the capture of Madrid's latest league title, he took some time out to sit down with your author in a restaurant near the city's Retiro Park and provide some insight into Jude's arrival, integration and impact.

'The coach here is not so involved in recruiting players,' says Ancelotti Jnr. 'The club has a clear line to follow – they want young players with big futures because they want to build a team. It's up to the manager to adapt to these great players. The club paid a lot of money for Vinicius and Rodrygo which was a bit of a gamble, but otherwise they just buy the best players in Europe. So they brought in Tchouaméni, Camavinga and Bellingham – all young and energetic players.

'Last season we already knew Jude was coming. We knew he was a really good No. 8 but because we were missing Benzema, we decided to talk to him when he came in.

We tried to explain that the ability he has to go into the space could help us a lot tactically. We suggested he play as a ten, as a false nine, to be free in attack, and he liked the idea. We knew the characteristics we had and we wanted to try this experiment with him. So we called him in and showed him a video of how we play. We told him: "The way you play could help us to have different solutions in attack." Jude is really intelligent. He understood and he was available to try. It worked really well in the beginning. Amazing.'

If Bellingham's ability to absorb information and accept suggestions made him a hit with his coaches, the way he conducted himself on the training ground was also winning hearts and minds in the dressing room. Crucially he made an instant impression with the team's leadership group, a five-strong committee headed by club captain Nacho and completed by Luka Modrić, Toni Kroos, Dani Carvajal and Lucas Vázquez.

'From the first training session Jude gave energy and ambition to his teammates,' explains Ancelotti Jnr. 'Even from that first session they said: "Okay, with this guy we can win." They were surprised about his size, his physical condition and his quality with his left foot and right. They were impressed with his quality as a footballer. Everyone. But not only his quality, the way he is. Because he fits into the group really well. To be honest this was not a difficult group to join because we have no superstars in terms of ego. We also have a good blend between experience and young players. The leadership group contains experienced guys but no egos. In the past we had superstars like Cristiano (Ronaldo) and Sergio Ramos, but this group is different.

So, for a young player like Jude, it was the perfect environment to come into.'

The Basque derby between Athletic Bilbao and Real Sociedad is one of the most colourful fixtures on the Spanish football calendar and one which draws plenty of football tourists to experience the inter-city rivalry of the two clubs. While there is a degree of tribal enmity in the air when the two neighbouring teams meet in either Bilbao or San Sebastián, the real hostility is reserved for whenever the Madridistas come to town. No club embodies the royal empire of Spain like Los Blancos and the sight of those all-white uniforms strutting on to the pitch is enough to prompt a visceral reaction in the stands. Bilbao's San Mamés Stadium may not be the bear pit of old, but it is still an uncomfortable stage to occupy as a Madrid player. 'It's good that it was Jude's first match,' smiles Ancelotti Jnr. 'He didn't know what was coming so he went in feeling not so worried.'

If any of that got under Bellingham's skin it simply didn't show. In fact it apparently served to inspire him. The moment of Bellingham's first goal for Real Madrid might have been an occasion for bashfulness. Having peeled away from the back post to meet David Alaba's outswinging left-foot corner, Bellingham showed a poacher's instinct for space. The finish bore fewer hallmarks of an expert gunslinger. Nonchalantly addressing the ball on the volley, his connection was an inch or two south of the sweet spot on the inside of his right boot. The resulting miskick sent the ball down into the ground back up high and over goalkeeper Unai Simón. Madrid had a two-goal lead and Bellingham was in no mood to offer his apologies for his good fortune. Facing up to a hostile audience behind the goal, he planted his feet in that familiar akimbo stance and unwrapped his arms to complete a four-pronged declaration of his arrival in La Liga.

'Tactically, that first game was also good for Jude,' explains Ancelotti. 'In August the teams are not so fit so that can make for an open game, full of transitions, a lot like he'd been used to in Germany.' He may have miscued that first salvo but in reality he was just getting his eye in. The floodgates were opening and he went on to find the net nine times in his first 10 appearances for Madrid.

There's nothing quite like the element of surprise, but Bellingham must have delighted himself with not only the frequency of his goalscoring but also the manner in which he was dispatching chances. Right foot, left foot, headers, tap-ins, angled finishes – forget the old '22' ideology. This was the skill set of an old-fashioned No. 9. And he was doing it at key moments in games. His winner at Celta Vigo on the second weekend of the La Liga season came in the 81st minute and established a handy trend of late, decisive finishes. Getafe took Madrid all the way in the first Bernabéu fixture of the campaign, but there again was Bellingham, four minutes into stoppage time, perfectly placed to convert Vázquez's spilled shot from close range.

It helped that he wasn't being asked to operate as a spearhead as such, instead acting as a floating threat from deep. Constantly scanning the pitch for space, he displayed an unerring knack of knowing just the right moment to hit the afterburners and attack the box. And even if the ball didn't drop immediately he was often in the right place for a ricochet or deflection off an unsighted defender.

Bellingham's football was speaking for itself, but his personality had also earned appreciation behind the scenes. At a club like Madrid there is often a fine line between confidence and arrogance, if indeed there is any discernment to be made at all. Bellingham walked that line with unerring assurance. On the pitch he was a tiger and occasionally a tyrant, turning his ire on opponents, officials or even a teammate who might not be living up to the standards required of this fabled club. Yet in private he remained unfailingly polite. And easy to coach. Four years younger than Modrić and just a few months older than Nacho and Kroos, Davide Ancelotti mixed easily with the players under his charge. Yet with Jude he was senior enough to be a mentor.

'The very first thing I said to Jude was that he should follow the example set by the leadership group,' continues Ancelotti Jnr. 'I told him he had the possibility to learn from Kroos and Modrić, maybe in their last seasons with the club. If it was only for one year then he needed to take everything he could from them. For us coaches this is a big help. We can pass whatever instructions we want but the real learning experience is with those experienced players. On a daily basis, Jude is really receptive. He is trying to speak in Spanish but to make sure he understands I speak with him in English. He is so easy to coach. That's not such a common quality. Not everyone has it.'

Some coaches demand absolute devotion from their players, proscribing a style of play that is akin to religious doctrine. Most famously and successfully, Pep Guardiola has constructed winning machines in Barcelona, Munich and Manchester through a clearly defined ethos. Players either get with the programme or they're gone. Carlo

Ancelotti works differently. Rather than force Bellingham to adhere to pre-determined patterns of play, the youngster was encouraged to freewheel and seek space on his own terms as he settled into his new territory high up the pitch. Operating as a false nine and supported by the rapid and tricky forces of Vinicius and Rodrygo on either side, he was running rampant. The role of Federico Valverde, the unsung hero of this Madrid team, in the adaptation process should not be underestimated. A tireless midfield runner, the Uruguayan was ferocious in his commitment to covering the spaces behind. A one man security blanket.

By the time it came to the biggest league game of the season on the final weekend of October, Madrid had lost just once – albeit in sore circumstances as neighbours Atlético prevailed 3-1 across town at the Metropolitano. Diego Simeone's streetwise Atlético team thrive in the fieriest of circumstances and riled Bellingham sufficiently to prompt a rash late tackle that earned the first black mark of his life in Madrid white, although surprisingly the referee opted not to show red.

Local friction may abound when the capital's big two meet, but the rivalry pales in significance next to the daddy of all dust-ups. There is no game in world football quite like El Clásico, a proper derby even despite the 400-mile distance between the cities of Madrid and Barcelona. The fixture list decreed that Barça would entertain first and so Bellingham's first exposure came on a balmy evening in front of 50,112 in Catalonia. Oddly, this was not the Camp Nou but the city's Estadi Olímpic, an arena normally occupied by Espanyol and, as with many athletics bowls, lacking the character and intensity of a custom-built football ground.

If Barça pride themselves on their left-leaning Catalonian ideal, there was still room for some rock 'n' roll royalty in the expensive seats where Rolling Stones Mick Jagger and Ronnie Wood were in attendance.

Would there be any nerves at tackling the planet's most fabled fixture for the first time? A little fear at being thrust into a key role in front of an almost wholly hostile audience? Not a chance. When it was needed, Bellingham grabbed this game by the throat. For more than an hour Madrid toiled. Barça took the lead early in the game though Ilkay Gündoğan and had hit the goal frame twice before the match swung. Jude had already matched his best league tally for Dortmund, the eight he'd rattled home in the Bundesliga the previous season, and so there was no reason to be apprehensive when he spied an opportunity to crack home the equaliser. Receiving the ball 25 yards out, his intentions were obvious as he knocked the ball out of his feet and lined up a piledriver that screamed past Marc-André ter Stegen. In the circumstances a point might have seemed like a pretty decent return, but in stoppage time there was Bellingham again, ghosting into the six-yard box to bundle Dani Carvajal's deflected searching cross past Herr ter Stegen. Off to the corner flag he went, saluting the coterie of Madrid fans perched high in the stadium bowl with that Messianic pose.

'That was the game in which he showed up,' reasons Ancelotti Jnr. 'Jude arrived in the league that day. Because it's the most important game of the season. Normally the first Clásico is in October or November and you can see where the team really is next to our main opponent. The pressure is not the same in the Olympic Stadium. The noise was not the same either. It was a little bit weird. The people were far from the pitch. But the fact that we won with him being the best player on the pitch in the second half was big. I told him after the game that I was really happy for him because he has come in daily and worked really hard. But he said that there was more to come.'

Jude's stunning equaliser against Barça may have been his best yet, but he arguably bettered it in Seville on 9 December against Real Betis. Starting the move wide on the left touchline, Jude moved inside with that rangy, flummoxing gait that by now had defenders petrified to make their move for fear of being made foolish. Offloading the ball sharply to Brahim Díaz, he immediately accelerated in a diagonal movement that pierced three defenders to meet Brahim's return chipped pass, controlling it on his chest and then rolling a controlled finish into the far corner. Just sublime.

Carlo Ancelotti is the undisputed boss at Madrid, operating with the aura of an old-school manager almost in defiance of his official title as head coach. At the head of his technical staff lies son Davide, born in 1990 when his father was a key midfield cog for both AC Milan and the Italian national team. The responsibility suits the younger man, but he is cognisant of the fact that the day is nearing when he will need to move out from under his father's wing. Now in his mid-sixties and with absolutely nothing to prove, there is also a sense that this may be Carlo's last job, certainly in a club context. During La Liga's festive lay-off – and Carlo being courted by the Brazilian FA with a view to becoming their new national team coach – Pérez moved to tie down his manager on a new contract until the summer of 2026.

The Ancelottis are realistic enough to know that it will be results that fundamentally determine their terms of employment. 'My ultimate goal is to be a manager and I think I am one step away from that,' explains Davide. 'I am in no rush because I am really happy here. We have a good team, a good group who are coachable. At some clubs you can sometimes feel like you are there just to name the line-up. Like you are an administrator. But if you have a group of collectibles like that it is time to go. My father gives me a lot of responsibility so I am happy. He delegates quite a bit. He works a lot on relationships, he talks a lot with the players and then just watches the training and steps in sometimes to correct. That is just the way he has to manage now.'

Not everything was going the way of Madrid's latest protégé, at least not in his own mind. Jude's frustration with officialdom had reared its head in Germany and was manifesting itself again through a growing card count in Spain. Through December and January he picked up six bookings in eight domestic matches and was also carded in his one European appearance against Union Berlin. Madrid's second trip of the season to face Atlético in the Copa del Rey was especially frustrating. Eleven cards were shared between the teams in a scrap of a round of 16 tie that went the distance. Ancelotti's team have been specialists in eking out late winners, but it was Simeone's men who came on strong in extra time, a piece of individual brilliance from Antoine Griezmann and a clincher from Rodrigo Riquelme prompting the Argentinian to charge down the touchline in celebration.

A three-game layoff to remedy an ankle sprain did not nothing to quell the agitation inside and it all boiled over at the conclusion of his comeback, a struggle of a match at Valencia's Mestalla Stadium on 2 March. There had been some poetic justice in the way Vinicius Jr had managed to haul Madrid level after conceding a two-goal advantage. Racially abused at the ground the previous season, the Brazilian raised a fist in defiance to the home fans as he turned the game back to level terms. There was controversy to follow as Madrid claimed possession from a misplaced kick from home keeper Giorgi Mamardashvili in stoppage time. Play was funnelled out wide and, as Brahim Díaz crossed, referee Jesús Gil Manzano blew his whistle for full time. The official had his back to play as Bellingham rose to head what he claimed was a bona fide winning goal and a throng of his teammates added their voices to the protests. In the end, Manzano decided to censure Bellingham with a red card.

Within an hour, the referee's official match report had been published online with Manzano explaining his decision to red card Bellingham: 'After the end of the game and while still on the pitch, he came running over to me in an aggressive manner, shouting repeatedly: "It's a fucking goal."' A two-game ban was handed down by the Spanish FA. 'I didn't say anything offensive,' said Bellingham a few days later. I didn't say anything different to what my teammates said and I think that sometimes, because I'm new, they want to make an example of me. In the end, I have to be responsible for my actions and I'm not proud. But I think two matches for that is a bit ridiculous.'

Nevertheless the incident was cause for a sit-down between manager and player where he was urged to calm his temper. Tellingly, and save for a card picked up in a friendly international against Brazil, he managed to avoid being booked for the remainder of the campaign. That's not to say his frustrations had disappeared. In certain moments during matches you could see the agitation when a decision did not go his way. And he seemed to have seized up in front of goal. After scoring a double against Girona in February he was sidelined for a month with an ankle sprain sustained in the same game. He would not find the net again for Madrid until late April but he found the most meaningful and dramatic way of returning himself to the scoresheet.

Four nights after a draining, stressful and ultimately euphoric Champions League night away to Manchester City, Jude was participating in his second Clásico, this time in front of an adoring home crowd. Going into the game there had been no little chatter surrounding his two-month-plus gap without a goal. Until he switched the ball from left foot to right and back again and unleashed a 20-yard shot in the 50th minute, there was little sign of the drought ending. Not that he was a passenger in an absorbing derby clash that ebbed and flowed, with Barça twice taking the lead before being pegged back by a resilient Madrid. A 2-2 draw would have suited Los Blancos by preserving their nine-point advantage at the top of the league table with just six games to play. Yet a game which had been played at perhaps 80 per cent of these two tired sets of players' maximum capacity had one final twist. And, despite running hard for 120 minutes and more in Manchester just a few nights earlier, there was Bellingham making one final, lung-expanding sprint in stoppage time. Lucas Vázquez did the set-up work, bounding down the right flank before smashing a low ball across the six-yard line. Substitute Joselu moved to connect but showed uncanny awareness to hold off at the key moment, his decision to let it travel farther and beyond the back post presenting Bellingham with his moment. His legs got him there just in time and as he clipped a first-time shot high into the top corner with his left foot he landed into a knee slide that was just the start of an extended celebration.

This was true Hollywood stuff, a thrilling climax to the derby to rule them all, and when he arrived at the corner flag he was met by Vázquez, the pair linking arms in a jig before *that* pose was rolled out for the first time since 10 February. Afterwards Ancelotti remarked: 'He came to us at the right time. He hadn't scored for a while but that could win the title, definitely.' On 4 May, Madrid clinched the La Liga prize. Bellingham climbed from the bench to score the second in a routine 3-0 win over Cádiz, but confirmation of a 36th Spanish crown arrived later courtesy of Barcelona's 4-2 defeat to Girona, the league's breakout team.

In response, Jude posted a solitary image on his Instagram page of him and mum Denise embracing inside an empty Bernabéu with the simple caption: *Campeones de España*! Much as Jude may have been keen to share the acclaim, individual recognition was round the corner in the shape of the La Liga Player of the Year award. A front runner in the league scoring charts for much of the season, his final total of 19 was overtaken by Alexander Sørloth of Real Sociedad and Girona's Ukrainian striker Artem Dovbyk who topped the chart on 24. Still, a share of third place with Barça's Robert Lewandowski was no mean feat and clearly impressed the panel of club captains, supporters and various associated experts. After his success in the Bundesliga equivalent a year previously, this was quite the double. Confirmation as a nominee for the 2024 Ballon d'Or prize would follow, as the rise and rise continued.

The real glory lies in the realm of the team and a Madrid title win demands a proper party. The traditional communal celebrations were delayed to avoid interference with preparation for the second leg of the Champions League semi-final against Bayern Munich. A plan was hatched for a jamboree on Sunday 12 May. On a high after easing past the Germans and strolling to victory against Granada in an inconsequential league fixture on the Saturday, Ancelotti and his players flew back from Andalusia and headed straight to bed ahead of an early rise. The league trophy was presented at Valdebebas before the squad, decked out in sharp black suits, headed into the city for an official reception at government buildings at the Puerta del Sol. There they climbed on to a balcony to greet the crowds below with Bellingham addressing the crowd in Spanish: 'Thank you for your support this season. One more big match at Wembley. Let's go to win. Hala Madrid!'

An estimated 500,000 people flocked to the city centre for the party and the team slipped out of their formal gear and into T-shirts commemorating the club's 36th league title. An open-top bus, also bearing the legend 'Campeones 36', then drove them to their ultimate destination, the fountain at Plaza de Cibeles where captain Nacho draped a Real Madrid flag round the statue of Cybele, a Phrygian goddess, and tied a scarf round her head before planting a kiss. There was singing – Jude treating the crowd to a rendition of '*Como no the voyage a querer*' – and dancing –

Ancelotti Snr summoning Camavinga for a reel around the fountain. The front page of the following day's *Marca* screamed '*Volveremos el 2 de Junio*'. We'll be back on 2 June. Indeed they were. This time with an even bigger prize in tow.

Chapter 3

THE SPORTING GENE

YOU could scarcely conceive of a greater contrast. The overwhelming grandeur of the Santiago Bernabéu versus the calm modesty of the Stourbridge War Memorial Athletic Ground, a giant field on which a future Real Madrid midfielder played his first organised small-sided games. Situated off the high street which dissects the town from top to bottom, it lies a couple of miles south of the now closed Wordsley Hospital where Jude Victor William Bellingham was born to parents Denise and Mark on 29 June 2003.

Home to both the town's football and cricket teams, the shared recreational space starts under a handsome brick arch that is easily missed from the busy main road. Yet once through the opening, one is presented with a huge sporting footprint, big enough to accommodate adjoining pitches and separate stands and pavilions for each local institution. The scale is impressive but there's nothing fancy about the facilities.

Off to the left on the southerly side of the campus sits the football pitch on which Stourbridge FC contest their home fixtures in the Southern League Premier Division Central. There are two stands with an official capacity of 2,626, perfect for spectators to watch their local heroes play. It's in front of these seats that Mark Bellingham scored many of the 144 goals he registered for the club between 2005 and 2008.

Adjacent to the football dressing room area sits a large communal space dubbed The Glassboys Bar which operates as a vibrant all-year-round community hub. The walls are dominated by a series of strips and photographs. There's a photo of Jude on the wall by the side entrance yet oddly no sign of Mark, the striker who once rattled home an astonishing 61 goals in a single season. Jude's potential may appear limitless, but there is one metric by which he is destined to forever fall short – and that's within his own family, never mind the wider world.

The goals have flowed freely for Bellingham since his move to Madrid, but even in the event that he 'does a Cristiano' and is converted into a central striker later in his career, he could scarcely hope to match the numbers posted by his father. The sporting CV of Mark Bellingham starts in his home county of Essex in 1994 and a spell with East Thurrock. By the time he signed for Halesowen Town in 1997 he was employed by West Midlands Police and his résumé then leads like a winding bus route of the region calling at Stourbridge, Leamington and 15 additional stops before terminating at Southam United.

It was at the penultimate destination of Paget Rangers that Bellingham Snr broke the 700-goal mark, a phenomenal output from a man who combined his penalty-box exploits with a career in the police. Teammates recall midweek fixtures in which Bellingham would run hard for 90 minutes and then sprint for the changing room to quickly shower, dress and present for the night shift.

Just as teammates and opponents found it hard to keep tabs on the striker, so did his managers. Such was his restless career path that he rarely spent more than a season at one club before he was on his way again. By remaining a moving target, Bellingham was also displaying financial shrewdness. The world of non-league football might not offer the riches of the Premier League, but clubs will fork out signing-on fees for the right player. And if your speciality happens to be scoring the goals that might make all the difference across a slog of a season, you're likely to be in greater demand than most. If you can bank one of these every other summer in addition to the monthly police salary, you're likely to be on pretty good terms with the bank.

By the time Mark started smashing in goals for Stourbridge in 2005, Denise was preparing to give birth to their second son, Jobe. Club president Hugh Clark has been involved at Stourbridge for 60 years, and his 25-year stint as secretary coincided with Mark's spell at the club. 'We didn't see a lot of him,' says Clark, almost wistfully. 'He always seemed to be one of the last to arrive and the first to leave. He'd drive in, park in a certain place and would then drift away after matches. You wouldn't see him drinking in the bar, not even for an orange juice.'

Mark would make rare exceptions for landmark occasions such as the end-of-season awards at The Glassboys Bar, where invariably he'd be picking up an individual prize for his goalscoring exploits. 'He scored 144 goals in four seasons, 61 in a single year which is a record in our 150-year history,' adds Clark. 'I guess he just had that gift of being in the right place at the right time. He was a clever chap. He was a policeman and worked his way into a fairly good post in the end. He moved around a lot – perhaps as a copper he didn't like staying in one place for very long. Jude was born near the ground and played in our younger age groups for a while.'

The boys would grow up watching their father's exploits and were inevitably drawn to the sight of him finding the net, making the difference and winning games for whichever team's colours he happened to be sporting on a particular afternoon or evening. If the goals were the moments to imitate and celebrate during their own kicka-bout sessions with friends and each other, it was the other stuff, the intangibles of sacrifice, work and duty that seeped through by osmosis.

The Bellingham brothers not only had a hero figure for a dad but a bona fide role model, one who taught them that nothing in this life would come for free – not a career, a penalty box tap-in, or a big transfer to the Bundesliga. Mark's dedication to the police was underpinned by an innate sense of duty to public service. If he wanted more for his own kids it would not be at the expense of the values that had carried him through life. Speak to many who have encountered him and they talk of a man who is fiercely protective. Someone who can come across as hostile in protecting the space around his family. It's no surprise to learn that a man who has served in the force would have a hard exterior, but the armour developed in confronting hardened street criminals is just as useful when it comes to fending off the attentions of opportunistic agents sensing the chance to make a quick buck.

Mark would not be the first parent to exert significant control over a child's sporting career and yield spectacular results. Californian Richard Williams harnessed the talent of daughters Venus and Serena and turned them into tour-ready tennis stars, a story that proved worthy of an Oscar-winning film. Earl Woods played a similar role in the rise of his son Tiger to the pinnacle of world golf. In the UK the phenomenon has been less heralded, but David Beckham's father Ted put in the hours to help his son perfect the ball-striking technique that made him a starter for Manchester United, England and eventually Madrid. All four ascended to the very top and both Serena and Tiger can lay claim to being the greatest their respective sports have ever seen.

So, in the world of high performance sport, where even a 1 per cent gain in any given variable can make all the difference, what weight of importance might be assigned to parental guidance? Call it a sporting extension of the nature versus nurture argument. The Bellingham phenomenon is interesting precisely because Mark and Denise are not only present, dedicated forces in their sons' lives, but because their father set a practical example for sporting success.

It's worth listing each of his clubs in historical order. East Thurrock United, Chelmsford City, Halesowen Town (twice), Cheltenham Town, Newport County, West Midlands Police, Sutton Coldfield Town (three times), Bromsgrove Rovers, Stourbridge, Leamington, Hednesford Town, Causeway United, Daventry Town, Bedworth United, Wolverhampton Casuals, Hinckley, Bromsgrove Sporting, Cradley Town, Paget Rangers, Southam United.

It's an exhausting list yet from Stourbridge onwards, Bellingham Snr regularly had a young fan club in tow, youngsters energised and inspired by the sight of their father racing off the shoulder of a defender to latch on to a through ball and tuck the ball beyond another helpless goalkeeper. The feeling of scoring a goal is often described by strikers as addictive. Well, that dependency can also be infectious. In that ridiculously prolific season in which Bellingham Snr broke the 60-goal barrier for Stourbridge, he allowed Jude to gorge on that very particular sense of satisfaction one takes from seeing and hearing the ball crashing into the net.

Gary Hackett, who played with Mark at Bromsgrove and later managed him at Stourbridge, remains a close friend. He observed: 'He could have played much higher, but Mark is a highly intelligent lad and probably realised his prospects were better in the police.' That didn't stop Mark laying a pathway for his eldest son, going so far as to establish Stourbridge Juniors, a team for Jude and his friends to mimic the exploits of the senior side. Within a year, Jude had been admitted to the Birmingham City pre-academy and Stourbridge Juniors died a death.

Mark continued to combine parenthood and policing with the art of scoring until he finally decided to step back. In the early hours of 14 November 2022, Mark tweeted to announce his retirement from the police force: 'As of midnight I became a civilian after 24+ years' service. Cops ain't perfect but they're trying their best under difficult circumstances. If we can show kindness to each other, we have a chance.'

*

Were it to be judged purely entirely on its own merits, the fledgling career of Jobe Bellingham would make him one of the hottest prospects in English football. Himself a Birmingham debutant at just 16, he was denied the distinction of being the club's youngest player only by the fact his elder brother had beaten him to the punch a couple of years earlier. Jobe's bow came in familiar circumstances, a cameo appearance as a substitute in an FA Cup tie against Plymouth in January 2022. Aged 16 and 107 days, he too was young enough to beat Trevor Francis's erstwhile record by 22 days.

'Young Jobe came on and looked so comfortable,' said his manager Lee Bowyer. 'He's earned that, he's been training with us for two, three, four weeks now, and you can just see him growing and improving every day.' By the end of that season he'd added another two substitute appearances to his CV in Championship matches against Preston and Blackburn. The following season he was a staple in Bowyer's first-team squad and played 23 times, most commonly from the bench.

Yet behind the scenes at Birmingham there had been changes that would directly impact Jobe's career path. Kristjaan Speakman, who had been Birmingham's Academy manager for ten years, was lured to Sunderland in December 2020. Less than a year later, Speakman had also tempted his successor Mike Dodds to the North East as he revamped the club's coaching structure at the Academy of Light. The duo's presence created an appealing environment for the Bellingham family when Sunderland decided to make a move for Jobe in the summer of 2023. Crucially, and in line with the parameters established when Jude moved to Dortmund, he would also be guaranteed precious minutes of first-team football.

The data-driven model introduced at Sunderland placed

a strong emphasis on youth and head coach Tony Mowbray was under instruction to flood his side with prospects of high resale potential. The club's signing policy had shifted to reflect this. Jobe arrived on Wearside in June 2023, beating a trail from the England under-18 camp where he'd been involved in three friendlies against Norway, Australia and Portugal. The officially undisclosed fee was reported as being in the region of £1.5 million and was announced on the very same day that Jude completed his move to Madrid. If there was a planned synchronicity around the announcement, Jobe was determined not to have his reputation entwined with that of his sibling. He adopted the No. 7 and rather than wear the family name on his back switched simply to Jobe.

'I think he's trying to create his own identity,' remarked Mowbray. 'He doesn't want to live off the back of his brother's name. He wants to be the footballer that he is and show people what he can do. He's an absolute diamond. He just loves football and wants to get better. He tests the coaches every day. He's a got a real growth mindset. At 17, it's unbelievable. Where he can be in five years' time I'm not sure, but I'm really pleased with him. His greatest asset is that he wants to learn.'

After his auxiliary role at St Andrew's the previous year, Jobe made a strong impact and was handed a key role in Mowbray's starting XI. Deployed as an attacking midfielder, his two goals against Rotherham earned the Black Cats their first points of the season. He would remain a mainstay for the duration of the campaign but the same could not be said of the men employed to guide him in this latest phase of his career.

Finding it increasingly impossible to marry the board's twin objectives in tandem with a proper promotion push from one of the world's most gruelling divisions, Mowbray would depart Sunderland in December (ironically being appointed at Birmingham weeks later) and in his place came Michael Beale, himself recently removed from his post at Rangers in the Scottish Premiership. Mowbray had steered Sunderland into the play-offs the previous summer but had publicly stated that winning promotion could only be regarded as a long-term project given the conditions placed on him by the club's hierarchy.

Perhaps naively, Beale fancied his chances. He'd been identified by Speakman and approved by the club's young French chairman and majority stakeholder Kyril Louis-Dreyfus, a distant cousin of the multi-Emmy-winning American actress Julia Louis-Dreyfus. Julia's roles in landmark shows such as *Seinfeld* and *Veep* showcased her flair for farce and satire, and so it was somewhat appropriate that young Kyril (he was 23 at the time of arrival) should find himself at the helm of a club that had proved such fertile ground for the drama junkies at Netflix. The streaming service launched its *Sunderland 'Til I Die* documentary series in 2018, taking a behind-the-scenes look at the club across a five-year time span. Anyone who watched agog at the dysfunction and calamitous decision-making that led to a culture of decline will be unsurprised to learn that the revolving door of the manager's office has continued to spin at speed even after the cameras ceased rolling in 2022.

Beale's candidacy was based on his record of working with and developing young players earlier in his career. As a youth coach, Beale had started out at Chelsea and worked with future England internationals Mason Mount, Reece James and Declan Rice before moving to Liverpool and helping the likes of Trent Alexander-Arnold develop towards first-team level. Although he too would quickly come to view himself as being in the wrong movie at Sunderland, he was instantly struck by the quality and presence of the younger Bellingham.

Beale recalls: 'The first few days in training I remember looking at him and thinking, "Wow." Physically, he is very similar to his brother – tall, lean and he moves well. I was super-impressed with his mentality towards training, his energy and effort and how he carries himself as a young man. He has played 70 or 80 games in the Championship now and that's a lot for a young boy.'

Although the family is nominally split into two camps, with Denise joining Jude in Madrid and Mark with Jobe in the North East, there has been plenty of back and forth from all four members of the Bellingham unit. Jobe's breathless schedule in the Championship made it hard for him to travel out to Spain during the season, but after wrapping up the campaign in early May he was spotted regularly in Spain, often posing up with his sibling for their respective Instagram accounts. Jude has found it easier to find time to travel to Wearside during the season. During Madrid's winter break, he turned up for the Boxing Day game against Hull City wearing what looked very much like a Sunderland scarf to cheer on his brother as he helped Beale's side record a 1-0 away win.

'It's a wonderful story for the family, to have two young boys who are professional football players,' continues Beale. 'Jobe is hugely proud of Jude but that works vice versa.

Jude came and supported Jobe as much as he could and was at a lot of Sunderland games through the season. Both boys are hugely talented. There has been a split-up of the family and that dynamic can't be easy. But they celebrate each other's success. Jude is doing things that a British player has never done at that age – winning La Liga and scoring in the Clásico, the big game. You can only judge Jobe on his own terms. If you took Jude away for a moment, I'm not sure how much you could expect Jobe to be doing at 18 years old. Last season, there was only Archie Gray at Leeds doing just as well as him in that league at the same age. This season he has scored seven goals but he has played in a lot of different positions and he is still growing. The knack of scoring goals from midfield is always higher value. Every team needs three and a half goalscorers. The pressure normally falls on the striker and wide players to score those goals, so a midfielder breaking in offers something unique.'

Beale believes Jobe possesses a similar technical skill set to his brother, and also the capacity to operate right across the midfield area. However, he expects him to move deeper as his career progresses – and his physique broadens.

'Over time he will find a natural position and I expect that to be as a No. 8,' adds Beale. 'He won't jink and dribble but he will run with the ball over distances. He has a good range of passing and shooting and those are the attributes he needs to keep working on. It's important he is playing in the Championship, where he will keep growing every year. Last year he was used as a false nine but he wants to run, compete and be involved in the fight. I'm expecting Jobe to get his man bones in the next couple of years and that's quite an exciting step to come because I have seen that evolution in other players. He is going through a bit of a growth spurt and in that regard he reminds me of Declan Rice, who broke through at West Ham at a similar age. At that stage you didn't always see the power and the athleticism that you are now seeing from Declan at Arsenal. At that stage your biggest concerns were his mobility, speed and athleticism, but now you look at him and he is driving away from players. The same applies to Jobe – over the next two or three years you are going to see his body fill out and he will become more powerful. And with power his movement mechanics will look different, he will move around the pitch more strongly and freely and he will be able to power his way through games.'

Jobe's zest for 'the fight', as Beale puts it, does come with a warning. Lukas Jutkiewicz, one of the senior members at the club, observed both brothers at close quarters as they broke through at Birmingham and shouldered some responsibility for mentoring each. In Jude he saw a remarkably well-formed individual, who oozed maturity from the minute he first trained with the first team. Jobe's temperament is not dissimilar but, as second born, he does bear a burden that Jude will never have to contend with. If the Bellingham brothers don't necessarily fall into the so-called 'heir and a spare' model that eventually did for Princes William and Harry's relationship as they navigated life in the Royal Family's line of succession, for the time being at least Jobe must cope with being known as a younger brother.

'Jobe was a little bit more hot-headed,' says Jutkiewicz. 'And he also had a bit of weight on his shoulders simply because of his brother. I didn't see any of that with Jude – he was just doing what he wanted to do and didn't seemed fazed at all. Jobe has had to carry a bit more with him and that is a challenge. Take it at face value and he is only 18 and has had a really solid season in the Championship. It's just that he happens to be related to potentially the best player in English history. Jobe could go on to play 500 Premier League games and be capped 50 times for England and he will still be in the shadows of his older brother. That's why I think moving to Sunderland was a good move – it took him away from that obvious link to Birmingham.'

Given how carefully Mark and Denise have crafted Jude's rise, the same attention to detail can be expected when ascertaining the next steps for Jobe. Inevitably speculation has already arisen over where he might head next. The football romantics have already linked him with a familial reunion at the Santiago Bernabéu and it would only stand to reason that Real would take a look at a young player who shares the genes of their current star asset. Equally there will be plenty of owners, if not coaches, in the Premier League who would be determined not to miss out on the next Bellingham after watching Jude escape to the continent.

Beale's involvement with Jobe may have been relatively brief – he himself fell victim to Sunderland's managerial promiscuity after just a few months – but he retains an ardent personal interest on what might lie round the corner for the teenager. 'I'm sure there is going to be a lot of interest in Jobe, just because of how young he is and how many games he has played,' continues Beale. 'And of course there is a value to the surname too because everyone has seen how well his brother has done. Forget the technical traits, if he has a similar mentality to his brother, that alone is going to be very appealing to big clubs. The one thing I would say about Jobe is he is not chasing the limelight – he is chasing being a football player. He wants to get his head down, focus, learn and be a model professional. Those are great assets because there is a lot around both brothers and the family. I was impressed at how humble the boy was. He loves football, it's all he thinks about. When I was at Sunderland he'd still be there late in the day, his mum arriving to pick him up at four or five in the afternoon. That's just him. Some players will leave at 1 p.m. But Jobe was 100 per cent dedicated to being a football player and that will take him wherever he wants to go.

'When you're working with a young player what are you looking for? Natural enthusiasm is so important. You don't want to be coaching motivation. You want someone who trains hard every day, stays out and does extra. Jobe did all of those things. He is passionate. And he can speak in the changing room which not every young player can. He's one of the players who drove the training. There were a couple of days where you had to say 'slow down a little bit' because you were mindful of the energy and mental strain the games were taking on him.

'The Championship is a gruelling league and I also saw some opponents try and go after him a little bit physically because of his age. It's not often that a second year scholar starts every week in a Championship team and at that under-19 age group he is one of England's best players. If you look at the current senior team and what those players were doing at Jobe's age, not many were playing as much as he has – his brother being the one outlier. We've never had two brothers like that in this country – certainly not mid-field players. Jobe's played at every age level for England but the comparison will be there until he breaks on to a similar level as Jude, whether that be moving overseas or breaking into the Premier League. They are both very clean-cut and focused on their careers. It's a wonderful success story.'

Jobe benefited from the guidance of a familiar voice after Beale's departure in February. It was to Mike Dodds that Speakman turned when appointing an interim boss to see out the season and Jobe continued to be a mainstay in the team. While Sunderland might not necessarily offer the best career prospects for young coaches making their way in the game, the chaos within the hierarchy needn't be an impediment to player development.

'The move to Sunderland has enabled Jobe to play week in, week out,' observes Beale. 'I don't know if he would have got that at Birmingham so that was a good decision. The family have made good decisions with Jude, first with Dortmund and then Spain, even if Real Madrid has to pick you rather than the other way round. When the time comes for Jobe they will have more of those decisions to make. Put the football part away and look at raising a family. I think the parents have done a fantastic job with both boys and they manage the situation really well. They are both really impressive young men. Jobe approaches you really well, with a nice smile on his face, good energy and a sense of humour. There is a lot to like there. As a parent, what more could you ask for?'

Chapter 4

LEVELLING UP

THE Bellingham family do not give interviews and, just for the record, politely declined to take part in the process of compiling material for this book. And so we can't quite be sure of the reason Mark and Denise settled on the name Jude for their first-born son. Perhaps it was in tribute to what has become his signature tune, The Beatles' timeless anthem 'Hey Jude'. Or might this specialist in dramatic last-minute goals have been named after Jude the apostle, the nominal patron saint of hopeless causes.

Catholicism features strongly in the ethos of the fee-paying Priory School where Jude was educated at secondary level, but an established tie-in with Birmingham City's academy system may have had more to do with that choice of institution. There could be echoes of religious faith in the paternal family lineage, as we know Jude could have been eligible to represent the Republic of Ireland. A picture of a young Jude in an Ireland top has been in wide circulation for some time and in the summer of 2023 it emerged that he had applied for Irish citizenship in order to avoid eating into the limited quota of non-EU players permitted at Real Madrid. A penny for the thoughts of those Irish fans already rueing the loss to England of Jack Grealish and Declan Rice, the latter of whom actually played for Ireland's national side three times, albeit in non-competitive games.

On the occasion of his Borussia Dortmund debut against Duisburg, dad Mark broke off from a threaded discussion around knife crime on social media site Twitter to say: '. . . it's been enjoyable but this half Irish kid is going to go online and watch his mixed race England u21 International son make his competitive debut in the German Cup.' Mark's pride is tangible and it's interesting to scroll back and read the tone of the earlier discussion. The thread starts with a Home Office tweet asking for opinions on a proposal to introduce greater stop and search powers to the police. Still a serving officer, Mark communicates with a persuasive combination of conviction and reason – no mean feat on this particular platform. Rather than advocate for those suggested powers, Mark outlines an alternative strategy, writing: 'Instead of concentrating on punishment and storing the problem for another day, look at genuine rehabilitation . . . it's the hardest option and requires a cultural shift.'

Mark's experience of working on the streets, communicating directly with youngsters involved in gang culture, adds weight to his words. And there is also a defence of the Black Lives Matter movement which gained traction in the wake of police violence in the United States. He adds: 'BLM is giving us a chance to be better. To accept the uncomfortable truth of the social exclusion of the black community and the inequality of opportunity for black kids before and now. Accepting the errors is the first step to finding the solutions and improve opportunities. Create a segregated environment in the first instance by ghettoising communities and we reap what we sow.'

Powerful stuff. And an indication of the thoughtful, principled environment in which Jude and Jobe were raised by their parents. The academy at Birmingham City may have served as the finishing school for Jude's football talent, but his character was moulded between two seats of learning. The home constructed by Denise and Mark in Hagley, a village situated just south of Stourbridge, was one in which love, respect and ambition were encouraged to co-exist.

Stourbridge FC, Jude's first football 'love', play in the Southern Premier League and take their Glassboys nickname from the industry which underpinned the town's economic and physical growth during the Industrial Revolution. A leafy place situated in the metropolitan borough of Dudley, ten miles to the west of Birmingham city centre, Stourbridge has for decades been a focus of West Midlands aspiration. In adulthood, Robert Plant would pioneer the stadium rock format as the frontman of Led Zeppelin. As a youngster growing up in Halesowen, Plant regarded Stourbridge as 'our Beverly Hills'. It was a place of comparative glamour next to the town he called home.

Mark Bellingham's rise through the ranks of the police brought him to the Midlands, but his career was never going to completely subsume his football. His identification number of 1966 told its own story and his continued non-league sideline offered a healthy release from the mental toll taken by the day job. Given that commitment it would be easy to assume that Jude was always going to be steered into football by his father. Not so. Denise, in particular, was eager to let her children explore their own instincts. And Jude was not intuitively drawn to the sport. 'Nothing happened until he was six,' said Denise. 'Then something clicked. Before that, if you gave him a ball he would pick it up and want to throw it back at you. He didn't want to kick it. It was a natural progression.'

There was a time when the elite footballer would typically come from poverty, a product of the streets where the ability to trap a soggy football as it kicked unpredictably out of a pothole was only as important as the smarts required to navigate the utterly human but often cruel politics of the street. The Bellingham brothers had a comparatively privileged upbringing, practising their sporting prowess on custom-laid playing surfaces and polishing their impressive social skills under the roof of the Priory School in Edgbaston, a fee-paying institution that routinely charges parents £16,000 per year for a place on the school roll.

Jude first attended Hagley Primary School, and it was there that he started to hone his ball control, although not without the odd wayward thrash. The school's former caretaker Mark Williams kept a pair of ladders at hand for these occasions when a Bellingham piledriver would find the roof slats and not the goal nets. 'He always asked you to get the ball down nicely,' remarked the janitor in a newspaper interview, which in itself demonstrated the insatiable demand for insight into the background of the school's most famous FP. Jude's manners are a common theme among accounts of the supervising adults from those days. His Year Two teacher Suzanne Shackleton recalls an 'extremely courteous and polite' child, one who was 'extremely dedicated to everything he did, not just his sport and football'.

James Ayers would take on the role of PE teacher at Hagley, but not before he'd sat down with the School Council to persuade them of his manifesto. Jude was, of course, among those pupils elected to represent his fellow pupils and straight away wanted to know what Mr Ayers would do to improve the football team. The teacher remembers Jude as an all-rounder who represented the school at cross-country and sprinting yet not every sport came naturally. When he failed to make the cricket team in Year Five, Jude used the disappointment as fuel for a summer of practice on the local field with his dad. When he returned for Year Six he had improved to the extent he was one of the school's best players and a driving force in them reaching the national finals. 'He had the mentality that if he saw someone who was achieving more, or was better than him at something, he would use that as the benchmark,' recalled the teacher. 'He'd try to be at that level – whether it was maths, English or sport. I would describe him as a quiet leader. He had a certain charisma about him that made people follow him and want to be with him.'

The move to the Priory offered a ladder to a new world at an institution that has sport at the heart of its ethos, affording it sibling status to its pursuit of academic excellence. The uniform of maroon-coloured blazers embodies a very British form of sartorial tradition. Anyone who has ever attended a Test cricket match at Edgbaston will know just how bucolic the area feels, its setting at odds with the tropes often attached with England's second city of concrete, urban sprawl and a mess of motorway lanes known as Spaghetti Junction. The school's outlook extended over-seas to the provision for international football tours. Ever wondered where Jude caught the bug to move to Germany and Spain at such a tender professional age? Well, that would have everything to do with the provision of trips to Freiburg and Barcelona.

While he was developing these international tastes, his place in City's pre-academy from the age of seven kept him tethered physically and emotionally to the local area. Bellingham would play schools football in tandem with his club endeavours and has remarked that the former afforded a relief and release from the pressure that accompanied a reputation that was already significant as he entered his teens. It would be wrong to state that Jude Bellingham was earmarked for greatness when he first signed on as a pre-academy player at Birmingham. Yes, there must have been *something* eye-catching about the way in which the seven-year-old manipulated the football in those early small-sided games at Stourbridge – but those who 'coached' the City kids at that time are more likely to remember unbridled enthusiasm than any ability to trap a size three.

By its very physical nature, sport is at the mercy of many more vagaries than an art form like music, where genius can become apparent at a tender age. Mozart may have been creating his first musical compositions at the age of four and touring Europe as a child prodigy at six, but young Wolfgang could sit down to compose without having to develop a response to a bigger kid coming along and knocking him off his piano stool.

Jude's arrival at the Birmingham academy was notewor-thy to his first coach Mike Dodds for the joy with which he approached his daily life. Dodds would go on to make an indelible impression on how Jude operated and carried himself, but at this stage it was the child's beaming smile that made the greatest impression. Speaking to the Blues podcast around the time of the Qatar World Cup in 2022, Dodds reflected on those early sessions. 'I've probably said this to Jude's face, but if anyone says he was destined to go and achieve what he has, then they are being incredibly naive,' said Dodds. 'I couldn't have predicted what he has done. No one could. Not even his parents.'

Dodds recalls Bellingham bounding around at training with a 'Tigger-like' enthusiasm. One day he might arrive wearing a replica shirt bearing the name of Zidane; on another he turned up with his hair shaved save for a little tuft at the front, a tribute to the Brazilian striker Ronaldo. These were not heroes of the time but of an earlier generation, a sign perhaps of further parental influence. There were also early signs of the competitive edge that was so abundant in Mark's non-league heyday. 'He would always let you know if he was unhappy,' added Dodds. 'He wanted to win everything he turned his hand to.' It wasn't until Jude reached his teens that he really started to stand out: 'He was very different because he wanted to be the best, whether that was in games, training or his analysis work. That's the one thing that always set him apart.'

Jude's transition from Hagley Primary to the Priory helped shape this work ethic. A tie-in between club and school sees Birmingham place players at the fee-paying institution that places physical health prominently on its prospectus. Downhill of the main school building is a patchwork of sports fields and, just beyond, a state-of-the-art tennis complex. It's all literally on the kids' doorstep, yet as he moved into his teens, Jude was being taxied off campus to Birmingham's Wast Hills training ground to join in training sessions above his age group.

At 13, he was playing for Birmingham's under-16s. A year later he'd moved up to the under-18s. At 15 he was with the under-23s and training with the first team. It was at this stage that Birmingham introduced him to media training and mock interview situations designed to acclimatise him to the variety of questions he might be bowled by a probing journalist. He handled even the most difficult of question with the same ease he'd show when riding the tackle of an aggressive defender determined not to be shown up by the new pretender on the training pitch. Not only that, he did so with an unfailing politeness and humility that continues to define his appearances in front of the cameras.

On the surface it appeared all to be plain sailing. During his emotional post-match interview after Madrid's Champions League success, Jude alluded to some darker moments when his prospects were called into question. Among the dozens of people spoken to, on and off the record, in the research for this book, none alluded to any doubts or difficult conversations regarding Jude. In fact the overwhelming message seems to have been one of encouragement. Perhaps there was an unintentional, throwaway remark from a teacher or a coach that stuck in Jude's mind and served as an irritating spur as he grew older.

Dodds, who remains close to the family to this day, would never have sought to undermine the youngster's self-esteem, but he did see value in making things tougher for a kid who could easily have strolled his way through the academy system. Speaking to the *Guardian* newspaper in May 2024, he explained: 'I've always said failure is a really important ingredient for success. We were always striving to make it really difficult for him, to challenge him and almost put speed bumps in his way.'

Dodds started to load training sessions against Bellingham. That might mean outnumbering his team in small-sided games. Or handicapping his team by packing it with trialists and less muscular players. There was fallout from those very obvious acts of sabotage. 'He didn't talk to me for three, four, five months,' says Dodds. 'Jude looks back to that period and realises now what I was trying to do with him. It must have felt like: "Why are you doing this to me?"'

And Dodds also wondered why he might be doing this to himself too, jeopardising a bond with a player he'd nurtured from such a young age. Denise Bellingham was there to provide reassurance to both her son and his mentor. 'She gave me complete autonomy, complete trust from the family,' added Dodds. Denise had told him: '"Just relax, be you. At the moment you two are clashing, but if you be completely authentic in this period, he'll come back to you and you'll be really close." Everything she said has happened.'

Denise was also reminding Jude of the importance of his academic pursuits. Bright and capable, there would have been a natural temptation for any teenage boy to freewheel through lessons and prioritise his football. Not in this family. 'We always said we wouldn't allow the football to overshadow his education,' said Denise. 'The education always came first. Both Mark and I said that if the education started to suffer then football would have to give. Jude has always understood that and luckily we have not had to go down that path.'

Birmingham's tie-up with the Priory School enabled the club to synchronise their youngsters' physical and personal development. Yet it's a fallacy to suggest that you can buy manners off the peg. 'I know the club has an affiliation with the school and I'm sure Jude benefited from going there,' says Birmingham striker Lukas Jutkiewicz. 'Having said that, there were many young players who went through the Priory and did not have that kind of mentality or respect when they came to train with us. His education helped of course. But his family have to take a huge amount of credit for that because it was the same with Jobe.'

'Mature is probably the best word to describe Jude. He was just a really emotionally intelligent guy. He came in to train with the first team at 15 years old and was holding his own not just in training but in conversations. His mentality separated him from the rest. Young players come up to train with the first team all the time. Sometimes they look like they are good but you never know how they are going to develop. Jude took everything in his stride.'

With his tall frame, broad shoulders and purposeful stride, it's hard to imagine Bellingham being physically bullied by even the strongest of opponents. But he grew at his own pace and while his talent developed at a precocious pace, his body took time to catch up. So when he was played up an age group, he had to be brave. 'That's what made me as rounded as I am,' he later explained. 'Having to battle for every ball, throw myself around and go into tackles where maybe it looks like I'm going to get hurt. Just to show I am fearless and belong on the pitch with any player.'

This rapid rise was being mirrored with England and the timing couldn't have been better for a prodigious talent to flourish. Gareth Southgate will forever be remembered as the man who got England to the final of consecutive European Championships, but he achieved far more during his wider association with the Football Association. Previously, a touring advocate for the FA's plan to introduce small-sided games for kids, the former international defender was appointed manager of England's under-21 side in 2013 and worked closely with technical director Dan Ashworth to sync the age groups and create a smooth pathway. Having St George's Park, English football's West Midlands hub, was crucial to aligning the age groups, housing the coaching staff under one roof and creating a collegiate environment where information could be shared freely and regularly.

It was Kevin Betsy, England's under-15 coach, who first took the decision to call Jude up as a 13-year-old in 2016, the year Southgate ascended to the job of national coach. Speaking to Spanish sports paper *Diario AS*, Betsy told the story of the scouting mission to watch a 12-year-old Jude play against Watford under-21s for Birmingham. 'At that stage there are no names on the shirts, or match sheets with the team lists – you have to identify players by their shirt numbers. If I saw someone very interesting I had to go and talk to the coach. Jude was the smallest in the group, I promise you. He was very slight, thin, but he went down to receive the ball from the goalkeeper, he had a vision, he could pass the ball . . . he was capable of overcoming players . . . and I said to myself: "Is that the player?" The coaches told me later that yes, he was Jude. On the way home I realised I had seen something special. When you are part of the formative stages, we say that there is talent that whispers and talent that shouts in your face, and that was Jude. I have only worked with two players with that generational talent: Jude and Jamal (Musiala). When you see him, you know that boy is going to be top.'

Quite naturally, the vast majority of England call-ups are given to players from the biggest and best academies. Birmingham were only graded as Category Two, which placed Bellingham in a minority when he was first summoned. The fact he was an under-14 operating at under-15 level presented a challenge in itself, but he was also being asked to prove he could cut it against others from the elite clubs. Aged just 13, he was understandably apprehensive: 'I was nervous, thinking, "I'm really good at Birmingham, against the teams that we play against. But how do I compare to the boys from City, Chelsea, Tottenham, Arsenal and United?" I go there, find it comfortable and you have that realisation that I'm not far off some of these, if not better. So I go to the next camp at St George's Park, closer to playing in a game. And I remember doing really well in the sessions and showing people it doesn't matter where you're from or what category your club is in, you can go and make an impact and show you're better than some of the boys from the higher academies.'

The team into which Bellingham debuted for the under-15s, at just 13 years and 171 days old, has aged well. Cole Palmer, Tino Livramento and Morgan Rogers – respectively now Premier League players for Chelsea, Newcastle and Aston Villa – all started while Bellingham and Musiala climbed off the bench at the same time in a 5-2 win over Turkey at St George's Park.

Despite Jude's own misgivings he was soon leading the team into action. 'He was the captain,' added Betsy. 'We did it on purpose, because we wanted to develop that leadership capacity even more. We thought Jude would make the senior team. That was the plan. What stood out most, beyond his football abilities, were Jude's personality and character. Jude listens and learns at the speed of light. As a coach, you explain an exercise to a player in September and you think that in three months he will have it polished. With Jude it will perhaps be in the next training session or game. The following year, instead of sending him to the under-16s, we kept him in the 15s, with boys of his age. The best tournament we had with Jude was the Montaigu Tournament, the unofficial under-16 World Cup. It's a very special event and we did a curious thing to motivate them. We asked all 20 of them: "Who is your favourite player in the world?" Some said Ronaldinho, others Zidane, others Cristiano Ronaldo . . . not one said an English footballer. Then we asked them the second question. "Who from here will be the next Cristiano, the next Zidane?" Because that is the level of players we wanted our boys to aspire to reach. At Montaigu, Jude did very well. He scored against Brazil and we finished in third place.

'In the under-17s, where he was also captain, we won the Syrenka Cup in Poland. I remember Jude confessing to me: "It's the first trophy I've ever lifted." Birmingham didn't win as many games, but they were focused on developing him. That was a really beautiful moment. He debuted with the

Birmingham first team and that's when everyone started talking about him. He came with us to the Syrenka Cup and grew taller, stronger . . . we had a very strong team, we beat Brazil twice, France twice . . . we were going to go to the Euros with him as captain, but it was cancelled due to Covid.'

The pandemic would only temporarily slow Jude's progress for after the resumption he was chosen for another leap through the levels, courtesy of a call-up to Aidy Boothroyd's under-21 squad. Environment was key and the transition was seamless. Formerly manager of Watford, Boothroyd first became involved in the England youth set-up in 2014 and stepped up to the role of under-21 coach when Southgate was promoted to the top job. No matter the role he occupied, the process remained smooth, familiar and consistent.

Boothroyd said: 'On Monday mornings we'd come in – all the national coaches – to St George's Park to discuss the game we'd watched at the weekend and the players we'd been out seeing. I'd be in with Gareth and Steve Cooper and we'd have a general, informal chat about what we'd seen and who could possibly step up if needed. That was never in any doubt where Jude was concerned and I advised Gareth to look at him as early as possible. I watched a couple of games and said he was definitely ready for us and we need to bring him in. He was going to be a top talent and he needed to be fast-tracked. Because of the quality and depth in the 21s, the question was how we were going to get him into the team. But because he went to Dortmund it made that decision easier. His mum and dad made a brilliant choice there. He was learning the language, embracing a different culture and playing very well, scoring and making goals. Everything that Jude ended up doing was thought out.'

For Dodds, his time with Jude was mutually enriching: 'I always said he was my best coach educator, because if he wasn't happy with a session or the route his development was going, he was always the first person to let me know his thoughts. He was always very honest and he has always been very driven. He always kept me on my toes during that period and it wasn't an easy upward curve for both of us. At times he probably didn't articulate himself the way you would want someone to articulate themselves, but that's a part of being a teenager. I've always said that because I was almost in the eye of the storm for the best part of a decade, I didn't appreciate just how good he was. It wasn't until I stepped away from coaching him day to day and I watched him play at St Andrew's, in the Championship, at 16 I thought, "Wow, this boy is a little bit different to most." He is just a magnificent human being. He is a role model not just for the young kids of Birmingham but now the nation. He has compassion, complete empathy for people around him. From a human perspective I don't have enough words to praise him. He keeps in touch with me regularly, he doesn't have to do that. He has said some really wonderful things that I will be forever grateful for. I think that just sums up the measure of the young man.'

Chapter 5

CITY SLICKER

FEW leagues in world football are as punishing, as brutally relentless as the Championship, English football's second tier. This context is crucial when examining Jude Bellingham's rapid ascent to the first-team stage. Excluding runs in the three sundry cup competitions or a tilt at the end-of-season play-offs, the 24-team division serves up a cruel 46-game format. The stakes are high, and promotion to the richest league in the world adds an almost desperate sense of longing to the mindset of the men holding the purse strings at each club.

Managers and coaches have evolved to cope with the schedule and that's seen muscle prized ahead of technical proficiency. Clubs build robust squads full of tall and broad practitioners and play the percentages in a bid to earn enough points so that, come spring, they are in touch with the play-off places – or at the very least out of the bottom three relegation spots. In short, you couldn't fashion a harsher environment for a teenage boy loaded with skill but still to fully grow into his body.

Relegated from the Premier League in 2011, the Blues had settled into a rut of accruing sufficient points to survive

while providing only the faintest of hopes to their supporters that they *might* sneak into the one-in-four lottery of the
play-offs. Quite practically, the squad had been filled with
physical specimens capable of running hard and battling
through the winter months to remain competitive. And so
the team's training sessions could be tough, testing affairs,
even for the most grizzled of pros on the books.

Striker Lukas Jutkiewicz had started his career as a
promising centre-forward at Swindon Town, cutting his
teeth in League One and League Two before earning a
move to Everton as an 18-year-old. After establishing
himself as a reliable Championship striker during spells
at Coventry, Middlesbrough and Burnley, he would settle
at Birmingham for whom he first signed on loan in the
summer of 2016. Not long after putting pen to paper, he
started hearing chatter around the club about a young lad
who was pulling up trees in the club's youth academy.

'We had heard the name but until he came and trained
with us I hadn't actually seen him,' says Jutkiewicz. 'It was
towards the end of the 2018–19 season and Garry Monk
was our manager. Jude was only 15 and he came to the
training ground in his school kit. He was only slight but
on day one he was phenomenal. It was quite strange to see.
You'd expect him to show a bit of nerves but there was none
of that. I remember the very first session. We were playing
a small-sided game and Jude shaped to shoot. At the last
second he did that drawback that you see so often now. It
sent our club captain Michael Morrison sliding off in the
wrong direction and Jude calmly rolled it in the other corner. It was one of those moments where you think, "Wow."
To have the temperament to do that at such a young age.

It was pretty impressive and, later, Michael and I laughed about it. But I have to stress how respectful Jude was at the same time. While he was almost taking the mick out of senior players with the ball, he would look people in the eye, shake their hands and say please and thank you. It never came across that he was trying to belittle anyone. He was just so . . . pure. So talented and just trying to do the right things on a football pitch.'

In years past, Bellingham might have been taken down a peg or two by senior players who would not take kindly to being embarrassed by a young upstart. Yet while the Birmingham dressing room was tough by modern standards, there was enough awareness and sense within the group to treat this gifted young lad as a potential asset. 'I think the game has moved on a little bit,' adds Jutkiewicz. 'That's not to say there was a conscious thing of going easy on him. Ultimately, if a player is being asked to train with the first team they need to show they are up to the task no matter their age. So it would never be a case of taking it easy. I don't think we were capable of doing that.'

Monk may have introduced Bellingham to the first-team environment, but he would depart the club in the summer of 2019. The manager's relationship with chief executive Xuandong Ren had been strained and tensions had only heightened when the club was hit with a nine-point deduction after a breach of profit and sustainability conditions. Jutkiewicz believes the club's Chinese owners – already eyeing a sale – were also pushing Monk to hand Bellingham a debut. 'There were murmurs of Jude potentially being involved in one of the squads towards the end of the previous season, but the manager chose not to,' reflects the striker. 'There was a lot of pressure to give him that debut because the club really wanted his value to go up. I think that was part of the reason why the manager ended up leaving in the summer.'

Monk's assistant Pep Clotet, who'd previously worked with him at Swansea and Leeds, was asked to take over. A career coach, who'd had a brief stint in charge of Oxford United, the Spaniard insists that whilst he was reluctant to take charge, he was in lockstep with the club's strategy to promote youth – and one individual in particular. 'There was a divergence between what the club and Garry Monk were thinking,' says Clotet. 'The club was in a difficult financial situation and there were only two ways out of it. Either we get promoted to the Premier League or we develop and sell players. Coming from a transfer embargo we were not prepared for the Premier League and that's what caused the problems with Garry. While I was assistant I never thought about being the manager. I didn't feel it was my project. But every time I go into a club I am interested in the youth set-up. And it was clear that in Jude we had a natural talent. He was playing with the under-16s but, technically, he was almost at professional level. He managed to keep his head high all the time. His touch, the control he had, allowed him to be focused on the game situations.

'At that age it doesn't matter who the coach is – the most important thing is not to destroy the talent, but rather improve it. But straight away I was of the opinion that we should promote him as high as possible within the organisation. It didn't make sense to keep him at the level he was at. This boy needed stimulus, strong opposition to keep growing. So when the club asked me to take over I thought, "Well, while I'm here, and I believe in this young player, Jude." We were aligned on that. But at that moment I also told them: "I will get you through the season but I don't see myself staying longer."'

And so, just a few weeks after his 16th birthday, Jude found himself checking in for a flight with the first-team squad, destination Portugal for the club's pre-season training camp. Alongside the intensive, lung-stretching work in the heat of the practice ground came two matches as part of a three-team round robin tournament involving Cova da Piedade and hosts Vitoria Setubal. The Estádio do Bonfim was the venue for this unofficial Bellingham debut, Clotet giving him a run-out in the second half of a game that kicked off in 30-degree heat and finished 1-1. The format of the mini tournament dictated that the game then went to penalties and, after each team had slotted away their first kicks, up stepped Bellingham. The first priority of any player addressing the ball from 12 yards is to get their shot on target and in this regard Bellingham succeeded. Unfortunately, his placement was anticipated by the Cova keeper, who pushed the shot away. Jutkiewicz would also miss – and by a wider margin as his shot sailed high and not so handsomely over the bar – but the striker was less perturbed by his own error than how Jude's miss might affect his mood.

'I went into the changing room thinking I'd have to console him,' recalls Jutkiewicz. 'I wondered how it might affect him but it didn't in the slightest. He was already thinking about the next game. By this stage we knew he would be involved a bit more. He had grown over the summer but this was the first time he had trained full-time with senior pros and he took it in his stride.'

The circumstances around Bellingham's competitive first-team debut were remarkable for the bold statistics rather than anything special that happened on an otherwise forgettable night at Fratton Park. Clotet's side had opened the campaign with a fine away win at Brentford and, prioritising the league campaign, it was an inexperienced side that was selected for the EFL Cup tie against Portsmouth a few nights later. Of the kids selected to start at Fratton Park on Tuesday 6 August 2019, Bellingham was the most callow of all.

Not since Trevor Francis's emergence in 1970 had a player this young been deemed worthy of a Birmingham City debut. Francis passed away in July 2023 but remains a figure beloved by the Brum family. Visit the club shop at St Andrew's on a match day and you'll find a framed portrait of the forward sitting on the shelf above the racks of replica jerseys. Francis would go on to become an England international and a European Cup winner with Nottingham Forest, but he also achieved wider historical renown when his transfer from West to East Midlands saw Brian Clough make him Britain's first £1 million player in 1979. Jude grew up with the tales of Francis's initial emergence at 16 and his subsequent years of loyal service. And so he made a point of sidling up to the club legend when opportunity presented itself for a photograph. 'Sadly many young players don't have a lot of time . . . they look upon you as has-beens and they are not particularly interested,' said Francis. 'So for him to show that interest – I respect him and I really want him to do well.' Francis was later presented with a copy of that picture, in which he estimated that Jude would have been around 12 years of age, equally respectful and ambitious in his burgeoning love for the club.

At just 16 years and 38 days old, and wearing the club's all-black change kit, Jude took Francis's record on a summer's night on England's south coast. Despite having few opportunities to shine in a 3-0 defeat, he earned the man of the match accolade in the next morning's *Birmingham Mail*. Reporter Joe Chapman's eyes may initially have been drawn to the player's fluorescent yellow footwear, yet it was how he wielded those neon boots that truly captured the scribe's imagination. Awarding a high mark of 7.5 out of ten, Chapman wrote: 'Boy didn't he look at home . . . despite his tender age, the 16-year-old was composed on the ball and flaunted his impressive close control. A real bright spark on a forgettable night. Tired at the end but this was a very promising entrance.'

Time has allowed Chapman the chance to reflect on what he witnessed that night. 'There had already been a lot of hype around him,' says the journalist. 'Arsenal had been linked heavily and had been watching him in Blues' academy so there was an anticipation this kid was going to be something special. He didn't let you down. He has properly filled out now and is obviously an absolute machine of a man, but at that time it was very different. He was very slender but, even as a teenager, he always had the height. Blues lost to a fairly strong Portsmouth team featuring a lot of seasoned pros, but Jude stood out, head and shoulders. I vividly recall that he was constantly asking for the ball. It didn't matter that he was just ten minutes into his debut or that Blues were losing at any point in the game, he just wanted the ball.'

Jude was played as an attacking midfielder and grabbed the game with sufficient force to leave Clotet surmising that not only had he been the team's main attacking threat on the night, but he possessed the skill and the character to make a meaningful contribution across the season. 'I remember a conversation between me and my assistant manager Paco Herrera during pre-season,' says Clotet. 'We discussed that if Jude could produce glimpses of these performance in league games we could be talking about a strong player in the future. He was destined to do just that. That was his level. Jude convinced me that we were right. That was his place and where he should be.'

Bellingham was not the only young player making his Birmingham debut at Portsmouth. Geraldo Bajrami and Odin Bailey were also featuring for the first time and, when Jude tired and was replaced in the 80th minute, his place was taken by Northern Irish lad Caolan Boyd-Munce, a 19-year-old who'd been picked up a few years earlier from Glentoran. The significance of the moment was lost on the midfielder, but Boyd-Munce quickly cottoned on to the fact he was sharing a changing room with a player wiser and talented well beyond his years. He said: 'I moved to Birmingham when I was 16 years old. Jude was three years younger but he would have been around us constantly, every day. No matter what was put in front of him, it didn't faze him. He wasn't quiet about it; if there was something he didn't agree with he would say it. He was just a phenomenal footballer. The things he tried as a kid, you wouldn't even think of doing. When he was 15, the senior lads said he was going to be the main boy for us this year. The only way to describe him is "special", and I used to say to my friends that he was going to be as good as Steven Gerrard. They would argue with me and ask how could he be at that level? Now they've seen him they know.'

Yet it would be rewriting history to suggest that Bellingham arrived in the Birmingham team as a fully-fledged first-team operator. After making that first appearance at Portsmouth, there was no sign of Jude in Clotet's next three match-day squads. A league debut arrived at the end of August, but his introduction, immediately after the third of Swansea City's goals in a 3-0 defeat, was of little consequence to the game.

The big breakthrough came a week later as Stoke visited St Andrew's. Named among the substitutes, Jude was primed for another late cameo but found himself afield after just half an hour when Jefferson Montero succumbed to injury. With the scores level and an hour still to play, Clotet's choice was a proper endorsement. And the 16-year-old rose to the occasion. Birmingham fell behind to a Liam Lindsay goal after half-time, but Jutkiewicz levelled things with a header, setting the stage for Bellingham to find a dream ending to his home debut. The goal was no classic. His low right-foot shot from distance was probably being covered by Stoke keeper Adam Federici but took a significant deflection off Lindsay and trickled into the opposite corner. Overcome with emotion, Bellingham burst towards the fans celebrating behind the goal and attempted a knee slide, which didn't quite come off. 'It's something I've dreamed of since I was a boy, scoring in front of the Tipton for my club,' enthused Jude. 'I'm very hungry for more. I've loved the club since I was seven. I can't wait to give them more of what I've got.'

Jutkiewicz continues to lead the line for the Blues but at no point in his career, far less his eight years at Birmingham, has he encountered a player quite as impactful as Bellingham. 'His debut at St Andrew's, he wasn't meant to play. Jefferson pulled his thigh in the tenth minute and if he was coming off we just assumed the manager would change shape and put someone else on. But he chose Jude and he scored. It's probably the scruffiest goal he's ever scored but it was a winner and it happened at the biggest moment for him.'

A week later, Bellingham was on from the start as Blues visited Charlton Athletic. And in the 52nd minute he showed intuition to hold his run until the last second before arriving at the penalty spot and steering Kerim Mrabti's cutback into the net to score the only goal of the game. This time, the celebration was slick and, in itself, a statement. Just before Jutkiewicz arrived to congratulate him, the No. 22 planted his legs wide and his arms up and out in a now familiar messianic pose. He'd arrived.

'Once he got a run of games you stopped thinking of him as a 16-year-old,' says Jutkiewicz. 'He was one of the team. We had to remind ourselves that we should look after him, not that he really needed it. He would be setting the tone, getting fiery with people and he was more than capable of looking after himself.'

In one regard Jude's age would not permit him to be one of the lads. With Christmas approaching and the dressing room in discussion about how to facilitate a squad knees-up, the club captain at that time, Harlee Dean, hatched a plan for the group to fly to Germany to let off some steam in the bier halles of Munich. Everyone was invited but, at just 16, Jude's involvement would have been problematic.

Jutkiewicz reflects: 'Jude interacted with the guys really well but it wasn't like we could say, "Come to the pub." We did discuss whether we should take him to Munich. Maybe we could talk to his parents and get a chaperone. The thought process was that in two years' time he was not going to be able to go anywhere and enjoy himself with anonymity. This might have been his last opportunity. The club were very keen to protect him and rightfully so. The head of academy was involved. Had they thought it was a good idea we would have spoken to the parents and maybe taken a chaperone. In the end we thought, "Let's not do that." The academy decided that the risk outweighed the reward. It would just have been one of the sacrifices he had to make.'

Common sense may have prevailed around the Christmas excursion, but Clotet was delighted to see the first-team squad so proactively keen to involve their youngest addition. Football may be a team game but the politics of envy and hierarchy that can disrupt any workplace are just as prevalent, if not more so, in the fickle and precarious environment of professional sport. As a gifted and rapidly rising star, and one not shy of sharing his opinions, Bellingham could have inspired resentment. Yet through a combination of his impressive performances, voracious work ethic and unfailing politeness in social settings, he was embraced by the older guard.

'There was something very fantastic about Jude,' says Clotet. 'It was very difficult not to love him from the beginning. In the difficult moments he had a total belief. Within the team and throughout the club, that got everybody's respect. He always had trust and confidence in himself and his ability and he trained on a very good level, never making the same mistake twice. In the locker room he was very respectful of the hierarchy of the players. He was very keen to learn the profession in those early stages and that won him respect. To be fair he had a fantastic group of older players who supported him. That was fundamental. The likes of Jukey, Lee Camp and even foreign players like Maxime Colin had an alliance with him.'

Fate would decree that the Christmas bash was one of the last nights out any of the Birmingham players would enjoy for a long time, but before the onset of the Covid pandemic, Blues found their best form of the season and clubs were flocking to watch the No. 22 in midfield. Coming through the festive period, Bellingham was in fine form, netting his third goal for the club in a rollicking 5-4 home defeat to Leeds United and another in a 1-1 January draw with Cardiff. The mid-season transfer window felt like a dangerous time for Clotet. Most fundamentally there was the risk that the club would seek to cash in on its young asset by encouraging an auction among the array of clubs flocking to watch this prodigious talent.

And then there was the ever-increasing media interest. Aware of the paper-thin line between confidence and arrogance, Clotet did fear that Jude's head might be turned.

'I thought that could happen,' he admits. 'Maybe the press would build him up if he starts to do well and he will lose his grip, his beginner's mind. In my opinion the most important thing for a footballer is that humble approach where you take on board everything from your teammates and coaches in order to grow. Jude never lost that and I was always positively surprised about the way in which he handled all the situations that came his way. In January he started to get a lot of attention from the media and the big teams yet he never lost his focus. I spoke to him a couple of times and he told me clearly that his place is Birmingham and he only wanted to help the team. He told me: "Don't worry, I'm here until the end, I am going to see it through 100 per cent." And of course he did.'

As the season moved through winter and towards the finishing straight, the world was on the brink of a truly seismic event. On 11 February, Bellingham's persistence in chasing down an apparent lost cause at Charlton would end with a goal-assisting pass for Scott Hogan. That 1-0 win was the last occasion on which he would experience a winning feeling in a Birmingham shirt. A 3-1 home defeat to Reading on 7 March was the sixth in a row without a win for Clotet's side and, as Jude trooped off at the end he could have had no comprehension that he had played in front of the Blues support for the final time. The following Friday the Football Association released a statement confirming that all professional football in England would be suspended until 3 April at the earliest as the Covid-19 virus started to spread among the British population. Ten days later, Prime Minister Boris Johnson ordered a full national lockdown, instructing all citizens to remain at home unless for specified essential reasons.

Football would eventually get back up and running, but not for another three months and the layoff had done nothing to improve the fortunes of Clotet's ailing team. It was a horrible time to be a Birmingham supporter but, oddly, Jutkiewicz remembers Jude growing in stature through one of the most draining spells he'd endured in the game. 'Just before the pandemic hit, Jude had really started to hit his stride,' recalls the striker. 'He was playing every week and was really on form. Then we had the break and didn't see each other for at least a couple of months. We came back in to train and it was like he had grown another three or four inches and also beefed up. I was like, "What have you been eating in lockdown?!"'

Clotet is not alone in feeling that his old club Leeds, then playing the high-octane brand of football prescribed by their Argentinian coach Marcelo Bielsa, were aided by the Covid break as they eventually secured the Championship crown and promotion to the Premier League. Similarly, he agrees that Jude benefited from the extended layoff within his debut season. 'Jutky is right, because Jude really did come back a different player,' he explains. 'I spoke with a physical trainer at that time and he told me the rest had helped him. He had played a lot of games. That sudden stop allowed him to absorb the physical load he had that season. We had a very good nutritional programme and he was working hard at home, but after the rest he started to become very dangerous in front of goal. That was the last step for him because it was the moment he started to become the player that he is now.'

By this stage, Jude also had a pretty clear idea of where he would be playing his football next. A visit to Manchester United's Carrington training ground had become public knowledge and Borussia Dortmund's name was also in the mix alongside Chelsea and Liverpool.

'Even at that stage it was a question of where and for how much?' says Jutkiewicz. 'He was just about to turn 17 when we came back for that delayed restart and we'd have mini games at the end of training sessions. The lads would talk about it – if he was on your team you'd just give him the ball and you'd win the game. It was that simple.'

Unfortunately the same rules did not apply when the serious stuff started. Football resumed under strict protocol surrounding social distancing and with no supporters in attendance. The first game back was a local affair, a 0-0 draw at title-chasing West Brom and that hard-earned point, coupled with another at home to Hull the following week, were to prove crucial in sparing the club the ignominy of relegation. The remainder of the campaign was a flat, joyless affair and, as well as he might be playing individually, Jude's own frustrations could be measured in the four yellow cards he accrued in the final six fixtures.

'The players were so lethargic and so fatigued,' reflects Chapman. 'You had 22 players reverting back to being professional footballers after three unprecedented months with Covid. Jude stood out. He may have known he was going to Dortmund but his commitment to looking after himself showed how incredible his mindset was. Blues only just managed to stay up, but Jude absolutely took the division by storm.'

On Monday 20 July 2020, two days before Birmingham's final fixture of the season, it was announced that the club had reached an agreement with Dortmund for the sale of Jude for an initial £25 million. His final game for Birmingham saw him come face to face with his old hero Wayne Rooney. By this stage in his mid-thirties and operating as Derby County's player/coach, Rooney bore little resemblance to the barrelling, dynamic centre-forward of old. Refashioned in a deep midfield role, the elder statesman was pitted directly against the young pretender who made an enduring impression. Speaking to Talksport a couple of years later, Rooney recalled: 'He actually man-marked me during the game, I think he was maybe just 17, and what I really liked about him was every time I passed the ball off, he'd leave a stud on me. I remember thinking, "He's got something about him."'

With a quarter of an hour remaining, Clotet signalled for Bellingham to come off and, in an act of imperfect symmetry, he trudged to the sideline to again be replaced by substitute Boyd-Munce. After 35 starts, nine substitute appearances and four goals, Bellingham's first season had come to a close.

*

Before each and every game, Jude Bellingham has established a ritual of wandering out of the tunnel and heading straight into the circle. From there he likes to manifest a picture of how the game he is about to play will look. The angles and possibilities that might present themselves and how the stadium geometry might assist him in his mission to control the game. Within an hour of the final whistle blowing on his Blues career he made a similar trek towards the centre spot, but there was no trace of the purpose and swagger which have come to define his demeanour. Instead, he painted a picture of loneliness, sinking into a crouch and drinking in his surroundings, not so much drowning his sorrows as giving them fresh saltwater to swim in. As he sobbed, the image was even more poignant for the lack of supporters inside St Andrew's. Jude had been welcomed into the first-team fray as one of the Blues support's own and now he was about to leave without saying a proper goodbye, the pandemic stealing yet another essential piece of human interaction.

Once he'd composed himself sufficiently he gave one final interview to the club's in-house media channel and all his emotion came flooding out in a most revealing summary of the season. 'To be honest the overall feeling is devastation. I can't help but feel that we have let the whole club down,' he said, immediately setting the tone for the kind of interview that wouldn't normally get past the censors of club media. 'The fan base, each other, the staff, the name of the club, what it stands for, we have let it down. We've had good moments in games but it's not enough. As much as we speak about it, something's got to be done and hopefully that does get done. Because at the end of the day it's my club. I'm a fan of the club and I'll be supporting them wherever I go and wherever I am. I just want to see everything go well and to be honest I'm devastated and so sorry that I couldn't, on my own, try and lift us a little bit to try and get us something out of the game and out of the last nine games. I know I have not been at my best but I have tried and given it everything. I have never stopped giving it everything.'

Here, then, is a 17-year-old boy carrying the weight of his home-town club on his shoulders. Close to tears he continued: 'We're a unit, we're one. So if one of us makes a mistake someone else has to dig us out. I've tried to create as much as I can, beat people, tried to get a yard to shoot.

The keeper made a good save, I hit the bar and it didn't drop in for me. I take full responsibility for that. I'll watch it back over and over again, I'll review that. Even if I can't do it again for this great club I know it's enough for them to know that I'm reflecting and looking at myself.'

The interview almost developed into a therapy session as the interviewer suggests Jude might be beating himself up a bit too much. 'Maybe but we're a team, and when the team loses, everyone takes responsibility. I'd like to think that I've made myself a big player at this club and someone who is looked upon to make things happen. I thought I had a good game today but I didn't get the ball in the back of the net, I didn't make an assist. I made a few chances, some good corners but if it's not enough I will be the first to tell myself. I don't really care if it's being too harsh or not.'

The earliest days of Covid had been marked by farcical scenes of panicked shoppers bulk-buying toilet roll. By the end of the interview at which Jude delivered a final parting message to the club's supporters, Birmingham's supermarkets ought to have been preparing for a run on paper handkerchiefs.

'I just want to say thank you so much for this season, for the way you have been with me, the way you have pushed me on. The little bit extra you have given me. Whatever happens I'm always a Blue. This is my club, I love the club to bits and I'd die for this club. I hope I have shown that in the performances while I was here. I hope I was fun to watch, to interact with and stuff because that's what I wanted to do. I wanted to bridge the gap between the players and the fans that had been there when there hadn't been an academy graduate. I will only look back on Birmingham City with love and fond memories.'

Bigger and irresistible challenges awaited. Jude had outgrown Birmingham, but his very departure did more than anything to ensure the embattled club remained in existence.

Chapter 6

THE ROAD LESS TRAVELLED

ON THE day Jude Bellingham celebrated becoming a league title winner for the very first time in Madrid, Birmingham City were relegated to the third tier of English football. It wasn't supposed to turn out like this, not after the sale of the club's boy wonder to Borussia Dortmund had staved off fears of financial collapse. Yet by the time American businessman Tom Wagner led his Knighthood company into a takeover three years later, the cash had been spent and the club was again living hand to mouth and reliant on a second Jude windfall courtesy of a resale clause inserted in the initial sale.

Birmingham had only banked such a chunky sum in the first place thanks to the integrity of the Bellingham family. For the duration of his year under Pep Clotet the youngster was paid just £145 a week, the terms of his scholarship deal. A professional contract could only be signed on the occasion of his 17th birthday and, eager to give something back to the club that had been nurturing both siblings, the Bellinghams resolved that Jude – and for that matter Jobe – would only ever leave Birmingham after putting pen to paper. Had that contract not been signed there's little doubt any of the other interested parties – among them Manchester United, Chelsea and Arsenal – would have been quite happy to take their chances at a transfer tribunal. Yet it's a credit to both the player, the family and indeed the conviction of Dortmund's recruitment team that a deal was brokered for pro status.

When the transfer to Germany was officially announced, two days before the Covid-delayed conclusion of the 2019–20 Championship season, Blues chief executive Xuandong Ren could scarcely have been more appreciative. 'I have to take every opportunity to express my gratitude to the family and to this boy,' he told BBC West Midlands. 'He could easily have just looked after himself and not the club, but he chose the best possible way to look after the club. We cannot possibly imagine, without Jude's decision, where we would be as a club in a pandemic like this.'

The Bellingham family conducted due diligence ahead of their big career decision for Jude. Wherever they chose to place him, the financial rewards would be bountiful. Taking a healthy view that money need never be a problem, they took a more rounded and holistic view of his career path. Development was front and centre of the discussion. Environment was also going to be crucially important. The facilities and trappings afforded to elite youngsters at the giant clubs of England's Premier League would provide a level of luxury on a level to which Blues could barely aspire. But there were also attendant pressures of remaining on English soil. And, given the waves Jude's emergence had already created in the media, there was also a real wariness of the pressures that might descend upon him as he sought to establish himself as a top-level player.

Early on, it was felt that a move abroad might be the wise choice. An opportunity to grow, develop – and make mistakes – away from the glare of a media and public who could well feel entitled to a piece of *their* next big thing. Yet all bases were covered, each invitation respected and often accepted as the Bellinghams advanced Project Next.

Most famously there was a tour of Manchester United's Carrington training ground just a couple of weeks before the UK was plunged into lockdown. Manager Ole Gunnar Solskjaer headed the welcoming committee, with Sir Alex Ferguson, an old master in persuading young players and their families that they ought to join United, drafted in to add substance to the pitch. Just for good measure, former United and England captain Bryan Robson was also on the premises along with the ever enigmatic and charismatic Eric Cantona. With such a seductive mix of personalities, United may have felt they were on to a sure thing. Not a chance. 'The most mature 17-year-old [*sic*] I have ever met in my life,' Solskjaer later said of his first impressions of Jude. 'He had it planned out. I was there, Sir Alex was there and Robbo and Eric were there just by coincidence. We all spoke to him and of course we sold it to him as well as we could. But he knew what he wanted; X amount of minutes in the first team.'

Weeks before that March assignation, Clotet worried that he was going to lose his prized young midfielder early. Scouts had been overwhelming the St Andrew's office with requests for match-day passes and the Bellingham family, determined to work independently of the usual agency movers and shakers, were fielding approaches just as regularly. They'd maintained a small, watertight circle with Mark operating as Jude's chief representative, and undertaking the necessary work to qualify as a licensed FIFA agent.

In such circumstances a club might normally be battling to hold on to its asset while the player and family agitate for a move away. Clotet found himself more in alliance with the family than his employers. 'There was never a moment when I got the wrong impression from speaking to the family,' says Clotet. 'They were always thinking of what was best for Jude but not economically. It was all in terms of continually growing as a football player. There was a fantastic belief in his ability from both his father and mother. That gave Jude a lot of confidence. And it gave us stability as a team. Because we were never dealing with a situation of a family thinking my son should be playing at Manchester United or these fantasies that can get into a player's head. They kept their feet on the ground. This was a project and everyone was working on it. One year and then let's see. Then the next one is to continue to grow as a player. That's a lesson for every family.'

While Jude was happy to remain part of Clotet's team, the Birmingham hierarchy were anxious about their ongoing financial travails and eager to realise maximum value from their prized asset. 'I never wanted to deal with a blow like losing Jude, but the goal of the club never changed,' adds Clotet. 'We knew we could not be promoted so let's solve our financial situation by promoting players. That offer could have come in January – and the club would have achieved its goal. I was always very worried that if that transfer option arose we were going to lose him. I think it's because of Jude that it didn't happen. He said he was going to see the season through: "I made my breakthrough here, it's my club, and I'm going to see it through." I told him I was always very grateful for that. In the name of the team, he stuck with us. Then when we started to do well and went 13 games unbeaten, we'd come from tough times after Christmas.'

In the spirit of full disclosure, Jude had also informed Clotet that while he remained intent on seeing out the season, he would be holding meetings with interested parties regarding his next move. And Clotet recounts an amusing tale that at once shines a light on the club's desperation to sell – and the player's sense of duty to his club, his manager and his colleagues. In January, United made an official approach to Birmingham and requested a meeting with the Bellinghams with a view to pitching a transfer offer. Sensing that a lucrative sum of money might soon be on the table, City's chief executive decided to facilitate the meeting at the earliest opportunity.

'One night, Dong Ren called me and said: "Could you reschedule the training for tomorrow?"' says Clotet, smiling at the memory. 'He suggested I might either move the session to a different time or even give the players the day off. I thought, well okay, it doesn't matter really because the team was in a nice run of form, it was the beginning of the week, a Monday I think, and I could give them the day off. But Jude found out. When he heard that we were trying to move the training for him, to assist in this meeting, he was completely against it! One hour later, Dong phoned me back and asked: "Have you moved anything yet? No? Well, don't. Because Jude doesn't want to go tomorrow, he wants to wait until he has a free day." And sure enough Jude went at another time, on an afternoon after training. That says it all, right?!'

By the time Jude heard United's pitch, German sports paper *Bild* were reporting that a deal worth a total of £30.4 million had already been agreed between Dortmund and Birmingham, one that would make him the club's most expensive signing ahead of the club's World Cup-winning defender Mats Hummels. Dortmund, and specifically their scout Sebastian Krug, had been trailing Bellingham for two years, but they weren't the only club on the continent paying attention. Bordeaux had compiled a detailed dossier on the midfielder. Juventus, Ajax and Bayern Munich were quoted in dispatches. Inevitably, Real Madrid too were alert to his talent.

From an early stage, Dortmund were ahead of the pack. The club's track record in developing then selling on Robert Lewandowski, Shinji Kagawa, Pierre-Emerick Aubameyang and Ousmane Dembélé had established an impressive player trading model.

Jadon Sancho had decided his prospects were brighter in Germany than in the overcrowded youth academy at Manchester City. And Dortmund were also in the process of persuading another promising English starlet Jamie Bynoe-Gittens, a year younger than Bellingham and still in City's youth system, that his career would be best served by moving to Germany. Already on their books was the prodigious and prolific Norwegian striker Erling Braut Haaland who had been lured from Red Bull Salzburg the previous January.

Dortmund had not always been viewed as Europe's premier leapfrog destination. Two years before Solskjaer's stunning stoppage-time intervention in Barcelona sealed Manchester United's 1999 Treble, it was Dortmund who stood as champions of Europe. And at the start of that historic campaign, the club had signed another bright-eyed British midfielder, albeit with considerably less fanfare. Already 26 years of age, and uncapped by Scotland, Paul Lambert had reached the end of his contract with Motherwell, who happened to have played Dortmund in the 1994–95 edition of the UEFA Cup. Lambert's comfort on the ball had caught the eye of the German club's technical staff and when he became available on a free in the summer of 1996, they made their move.

Yet his signing was an anomaly. 'At that time, Dortmund was not a development club,' Lambert recalls. 'I walked into a room with Stefan Reuter, Jürgen Kohler, both World Cup and Serie A winners. We had Júlio César and Matthias Sammer. Paulo Sousa was the reigning Serie A player of the year. Michael Zorc had scored goals for fun. The quality was bang in your face. Everybody. I was the only non-international! Now it's different. Mats Hummels, great. But there's only one or two in that bracket.

Back then it was geared to win, win, win. Lambert said: 'Dortmund don't generate the same revenue as Bayern Munich through corporate sales etc. because the stadium is not built for that. If you want luxury go to Bayern. But if you want a proper atmosphere and you want to see a game of football, it's Dortmund. Everybody in the world wants to go to their games because of what you see in the stadium. As for Jude's decision to go there? Whoever made the decision, whether it was Jude or his mum and dad, it was an absolute master stroke.'

Dortmund's transfer strategy had been overseen by Lambert's former teammate Zorc, who had moved into the role of sporting director following his retirement from playing in 1998.

Yet the man credited with facilitating the club's game-changing switch in emphasis was chief scout Sven Mislintat, known as the 'Diamond Eye'. After 11 productive years, Mislintat had moved on to Arsenal in 2017 and his bejewelled eye was well aware of Bellingham's accelerated progress through the ranks with both England and Birmingham. Sources close to Arsenal insist he had been fostering the links that would facilitate a move for Bellingham even before his breakthrough season. Crucially, and perhaps fortuitously for Dortmund, their old talent-spotter departed North London for Stuttgart in April 2019. Carefully, and over a period of many months, the Bellinghams examined their choices. The easy option would have been to stay local, in relative terms. Manchester United's offer accentuated the positives of joining an elite institution, all within easy reach of the comforts of home.

Yet the magic that enveloped Old Trafford in the days when Sir Alex was able to lure the likes of David Beckham from London or even Cristiano Ronaldo from Portugal had worn off. The Scot's retirement in 2013 had set in chain a long decline at a club that had come to define success in the previous 20 years of the Premier League era. And, anyway, the Bellingham family were not interested in instant gratification, be that through money or access to the luxuries bestowed upon young players primed to make the big breakthrough into the self-styled 'best league in the world'. The Bellinghams have always thought differently.

And Dortmund too had evolved from their old ways to best maximise their prospects in this new age of the super-clubs. By altering the club model from end destination to a super-sized stepping stone, the club was able to position itself as the premier finishing school for the world's best talent. And, crucially, there was already an English example *in situ* in the shape of Sancho. Lambert has loved watching this new Dortmund emerge.

'I was older, but moving abroad made me grow up really quickly,' he says. 'You have to take responsibility both in your football and in your life and it all happens really quickly. When I say it was a master stroke I mean that Jude would not have developed at the same rate elsewhere. For a start he might not have had the game time. And if he'd stayed in Britain my gut feeling is he'd just be another name. At Dortmund he was catapulted towards stardom and a lot of that is down to Edin Terzić who was the perfect coach for him, a young guy and a Dortmund fan too. You could maybe have seen Jude develop at the same rate under Pep Guardiola or maybe Jürgen Klopp. But I'm not sure the culture in Britain would have allowed him to develop into the player he is now. His mum and dad saw the benefit of getting him out of the British environment. And he was going to play in front of 80,000 people. Outside Wembley, no stadium in Britain can match that.'

Clotet, whose coaching pathway had brought him from Spain to Britain through stints in Sweden and Norway, had experienced the character-forming benefits of working and living in different cultures. And so he too endorsed the family's decision to take Jude outside of the UK. 'At that time I felt it was the right choice and the programme steps which the family had in mind were always intended to take him somewhere he could grow. Playing time was important too, but Jude and the family never pushed in a way where they demanded that guarantee. The only insistence was that they would have the chance to show how good he is, that he had an opportunity to prove he could belong and continue to grow. The Bundesliga was a different league. Dortmund were having a lot of experience with young players. There might have been a desire to go to a big English club, but this was the right step and I understood it perfectly. It aligned perfectly with what I knew about him and the family.'

And so Dortmund won the prize of the Bellingham signature. Concluded in Covid times, the deal was already subject to some unusual conditions, yet there was added theatre in the way his arrival was executed. With far fewer planes in the sky it wasn't difficult to track the player's arrival, so there was plenty of media on the scene to intercept the world's most expensive 17-year-old. In response, Dortmund assembled a welcoming committee to meet the aircraft as it offloaded its precious cargo and, legend has it, sent four identical vehicles speeding off from the airport each in a different direction to outfox the hungry pack. One can only imagine the sense of fun a teenager might take in such an episode of subterfuge, but there was a serious side to this next stage of the 'programme'. Not only would Jude have to acclimatise to his new environment within the sterile conditions of a pandemic, but there would also be a necessary split in the family unit.

It was decided that Denise would make the move to Germany with her eldest, with Mark remaining in

Stourbridge with Jobe as he continued his own ascent through the Blues ranks. This division of resources, eased first by the lifting of pandemic restrictions, and later by the growing independence of Jude, required sacrifice and resolve from all parties. That the four still seem as close as ever when they regularly convene in public at either sibling's games, speaks to something quite admirable. It may never be possible to know the precise dynamics of the family unit – and frankly is it really anyone else's business? – but there's clearly something worth learning from the playbook of Team Bellingham.

That protective environment would be important at Jude's new club as he moved away from the paternal influences of the likes of Clotet and Dodds. The notion of a head coach or manager not having full control of transfer matters remains anathema to the traditionalists of British football, but in Germany the trainer is there to do just that. Lucien Favre would not be in charge of Jude for long, and indeed the Swiss coach's departure would introduce him to an influential new relationship with Edin Terzić. Yet for the first weeks, Jude had to prove himself to a coach who had little if any involvement in selecting him to play for his new club.

'Maybe in Britain it is a little bit different,' says journalist and broadcaster Oliver Müller, who covers Dortmund for the Sport1 television channel. 'In Germany, and especially at Dortmund, the decisions are made more by the technical board. So at the time it was down to Michael Zorc and in previous years someone like Sven Mislintat who did all the work in researching those players. Michael said to me: "We can convince players just by showing our team sheets from last season. They will see that not only are they coming to Dortmund but they will get the chance play in the Bundesliga and also the Champions League." When Jude Bellingham came to Dortmund the coach was Lucien Favre, who I'm not sure would even have known the name before it was presented to him. Of course he quickly came to realise he has a great talent.'

For the first months of his Dortmund career, Jude was denied the full Westfalen experience as the stadium lay empty save for a scattering of club employees, media and essential staff. As they tuned in to their welcome helping of remote action, it didn't take long for the Dortmund fans to warm to their new signing.

'It's quite a special thing that Borussia Dortmund is able to bring in so many young and talented international players,' says Müller. 'The advantage of that strategy is they develop, help the club play really good football and then in a couple of years are sold for much more money. The disadvantage is that the chance for supporters to identify with these players is not so big. For example, you buy a shirt with Erling Haaland on the back, you fall in love with the player, and then two and a half years later he moves away. With Jude you could quickly see that he would not stay very long, but his style of play, the way he played, the emotions involved, that was something that really touched the supporters in a way.'

The Dortmund fans quickly identified with the dynamic youngster wearing 22 on the back of his bright yellow jersey. Meanwhile, 400 miles away, a man was making waves with his decision to withdraw the number from circulation. Perhaps carried away on the euphoria of closing the lifesaving Bellingham deal, Xuandong Ren made the executive decision to retire Birmingham City's No. 22 jersey. From the outside this gesture looked overly dramatic if not downright odd. Retiring a shirt is akin to erecting a statue or naming a stand, a definitive gesture towards esteemed figures who have given sustained service. More often than not, these legends will also have passed on from this life. Honouring a teenager in perpetuity seemed performative. After all, the club had never made a similar tribute to Trevor Francis, a towering Blues figure who'd delivered several years of service before delivering his own record transfer sum.

CEO Ren sought to clarify the club's intentions, insisting Jude's jersey was merely being mothballed in anticipation of a future return: 'Look, first of all it wasn't a retirement. I think reserve is more like it. He is a Birmingham City boy. In two, three years when we are in the Champions League, we might want him back.' A degree in economics was not necessary to dismiss Ren's words as ridiculous. The sale of Bellingham may have chased the wolves from the door, but the threat of financial calamity lurked in the neighbouring trees. After another season flirting with relegation, Ren resigned his position. And supporters were left more worried than ever about the future direction of their club. Bellingham himself had been left initially perplexed by the decision to withdraw his shirt. Speaking to *L'Équipe* a few years later he remarked: 'They told me, "No one will take it back until you get back to Birmingham." I was like, "Really?" I had a good year but it was nothing extraordinary. But I understand the position and the decision. My transfer saved the club which was in a difficult position.'

The danger was not over. And it was not until the club received that second Bellingham windfall in the summer of 2023 that it started to move forward under new ownership. It had taken New York-based financier Wagner several attempts to get his deal over the line. Aware of the disconnect between the club's Chinese powerbrokers and fan base, he'd set up a takeover vehicle entitled Shelby Companies Ltd. For the uninitiated, Shelby is the surname of the Birmingham-based family around which the popular BBC drama series *Peaky Blinders* revolves. Wagner was clearly intent on fostering a connection with the city but, for all his fresh promises, he was still beholden to the EFL's financial rules. Reports on the exact percentage of the sell-on clause brokered in the sale of Jude to Dortmund have varied, but a substantial sum – most commonly estimated at around £6 million – made its way to the Midlands when Madrid paid their fee. A relieved Wagner did not try to hide the significance of that clause as he set to work. He said: 'The reality is prior ownership was counting on that sale for a period of time, so much of those funds were effectively spent in the past. (It) helps us avoid a potential penalty for excessive losses. We're thankful because it helped us to avoid a situation that could have been rather untenable.'

Blues fans harbouring suspicions over this latest instalment of overseas ownership were at least partly won over by Wagner's big-league sporting credentials. Within weeks it was announced that NFL great Tom Brady had invested in the club and had been appointed as chairman to the club's new advisory board. Soon the seven-time Super Bowl champion was visiting St Andrew's and talking up the prospects of the club ascending to England's elite. Head coach

John Eustace, who'd been in charge for a year and avoided relegation with room to spare the previous season, would have seen the writing on the wall. But the decision to sack him after 11 games of the new campaign was an especially crass move. With the team sitting in a healthy sixth position in the Championship table, a statement was released citing a need for 'alignment' between the board and the manager, incorporating a 'no fear' playing style under the next boss.

Wayne Rooney was an eye-catching appointment and one that would have intrigued Jude as he settled into his new life in Spain. Yet what followed was excruciating. In the six games it took Rooney to chalk up his first win, Blues were tumbling down the league ladder. He'd win just one more before being sacked in November, just 15 games and 83 days since his appointment. The team sat 20th in the table. The board moved quickly to recruit Tony Mowbray, but although the side's fortunes immediately improved under his wise and proven tutelage, illness would soon force the former Sunderland boss to step down, leaving Gary Rowett in interim charge. Relegation was confirmed on the final day of the season on a sunny afternoon at St Andrew's, where an odd sort of atmosphere surrounded the supporters prior to kick-off. There was no real confidence that the team would avoid its fate but it was possible to detect cautious optimism for the future.

In Madrid you can't move for supporters sporting the No. 5 jersey of their club's latest superstar but, despite the gesture of retiring Bellingham's number, there is no obvious effort being made to cash in on his legacy. The club shop offers a number-printing facility and while staff admit to receiving the odd request for 22, there was greater pro-liferation of 'Caddis 31' on the pavements outside. Those in the know will get the reference to the Scottish full-back Paul Caddis, who saved the club from relegation with a stoppage-time goal on the final day of the season in 2014. On the side of the shop there is a mural, dually dedicated to Trevor Francis and Bellingham. Daubed in several shades of blue there are three images of each, including celebra-tion shots that depict the 8 on Francis's back and Jude's 22. 'Record Breakers' it declares, alongside the slogan 'we're in this together' astride the letters KRO, shorthand for the club anthem 'Keep Right On'.

Round the corner there's a solitary image of Brady eye-ing up a pass in his Patriots attire. It looks sparse and lonely by comparison. All of this could be pulled down if Brady and Wagner succeed in Knighthood's mission to construct a new, purpose-built arena in the city. For now, the visual tribute to Bellingham is a magnet for fans looking for a match-day selfie or Instagram post and its appeal stretches beyond the locals. Norwich fan James Tipple stopped by with his son Josh to have their picture taken at the mural, saying: 'For me he is the perfect role model for any aspiring kids. He's reached a level in the game where he's as much an influence off the field as on it. It's hard to find that level of professionalism and he shows a similar level of character to Ronaldo and Messi. He is a future Ballon d'Or winner for me. Let's hope he hasn't done too much too soon like we've seen with other English talents . . .'

Sam Daniels, a Blues fan in his early thirties, also stops by for a pic and a chat: 'It's just pride that someone from our club has reached that level. He is still a supporter. A lot of people might push that away when they get to a certain level, but he is proud of where he came from. At the time everyone mocked us for retiring the jersey, especially our slightly noisier neighbours, but it might just come back round. All the Blues fans still follow him. It's the same as Trevor Francis really. Although he left and went on to Nottingham Forest, he still felt like a Blues player. I'd love Jude to come back, maybe not in League One! Maybe when he is 55 and we can put him on for the last five minutes . . .'

Perhaps there is a master plan for Jude to return to his roots before he finishes playing, but it's difficult to see a reason for him to leave Madrid anytime soon. If England's top tier is a future destination, the big guns will doubtless be in competition. But if Birmingham's new owners follow through one of their grand promises – and that remains a giant if – then there could be an emotional pull towards his home club.

'Relegation is always difficult to take, but there's optimism for what is to come,' says *Birmingham Mail*'s Chapman. 'If Blues had been relegated under the previous owners this would have been an utter disaster. They'd be in a really perilous situation. It's fair enough to say that Jude pretty much saved the club just by doing enough to catch the eye of European heavyweight teams. You only have to hear him talk to know he's a proper Bluenose and there is only goodwill and adoration from the fans. Everybody realises he is a genuine Birmingham City fan who unknowingly rescued the club. At the time it seemed farcical to save the shirt, but maybe they got that right the way his career has gone. Maybe in his mid-thirties he might return and pick it up again. Being who he is, he would probably quite like to do that. These owners seem very serious. They have bought an enormous amount of land in Birmingham to build the new stadium, which they want built by 2029. You'll still find sceptics, but if this all comes to fruition, things could be exciting. They could potentially walk League One this year and come back even stronger. You can't see Jude leaving Madrid anytime soon. And if he did I'm sure City, United, Arsenal or Liverpool would take him.'

Chapter 7

SCALING THE YELLOW WALL

THE newest branch of Lotte's Curry emporium occupies a corner space on a pretty nondescript street to the north-west of Dortmund's city centre. Yet it was here at 60 Oesterholzstrasse, within the premises formerly known as Der Wildschütz Tavern, that Borussia Dortmund was formed in 1909. A plaque on the wall outside denotes this little piece of football history and inside, the restaurant continues to uphold its connection to the club with an impressive seating area painted in the striking black and yellow colours of the club. Festooning the walls and shelves are all manner of shirts, pictures and assorted memorabilia dedicated to the club.

Dortmund have long since abandoned the Borsigplatz neighbourhood for the land on which the Westfalen Stadium sits south of the city centre, two and a half miles away. Yet the locals are proud of their football heritage. Most people are in this proud, industrial city. The restaurant's current manager, Klaus Klinger, only took over in the weeks leading up to Euro 2024. After serving up a lunchtime portion of the house special of currywurst and pommes frites (German sausage, a sweet curry sauce and chips), he articulated his determination to maintain the shop's links to the past. As manager of a chain restaurant he understands better than anyone that the concerns of commerce too often override tradition. Nevertheless, he regards his particular franchise as special. Just as he will fight to maintain the integrity of his restaurant so he hopes Dortmund can maintain their relevance as a club within the European elite.

Mention of Jude Bellingham raises a smile as three years' worth of memories dance in the mind. Yet the transfer of a rising star, still a teenager when the decision was taken to cash in and let him move to Real Madrid, highlights a wider problem for anyone trying to protect tradition over money. 'Jude was great, but he was here for too short a time,' he says earnestly. 'Bellingham, Haaland, Dembélé – we are too small for these players. A big club yes, with tradition, but we don't have the money. We are a stepping stone. But we are good for these players.'

It was in the Swiss spa resort of Bad Ragaz that Jude Bellingham was first introduced to the German media in the summer of 2020. At first glance, broadcaster Oliver Müller wondered if he'd been wrongly assigned to cover the youth team's training camp. 'Jude was presented to some journalists and I thought not only is he 17 but he looks it too! He told us a little bit about his life, his development so far and his expectations. I was not sure if they might put him in the youth department, but straight away he was in the squad for the Bundesliga.'

Any doubts over Bellingham's capacity to adapt dissolved instantly. That crucial promise of game time was delivered by Dortmund's Swiss manager Lucien Favre and the teenager repaid in bundles. His Dortmund debut arrived on 14 September, in a German Cup match away at Duisburg. Favre set the team up to attack, with Bellingham operating in a midfield three alongside Emre Can and Giovanni Reyna. By half-time they were three goals to the good, with Bellingham netting his first goal on German soil in the 30th minute, accepting Thorgan Hazard's flick and forcing his shot through the opposing goalkeeper. Still operating under Covid restrictions, Bellingham had no spectators to interact with and instead raised an arm before pointing at his chest as if to inform the cameras that they had better get used to focusing their lenses in his direction.

On match day one of the league season he registered his first assist in another comfortable win over Borussia Mönchengladbach. Teammate Thomas Delaney, a Danish international, was immediately struck by Bellingham's personality. 'He was intense,' said Delaney, who went on to play for Hoffenheim in the summer of 2021. 'Sometimes you'd forget he was 17. And he forgot it too! He was someone I loved to play with – and hate to play against. He doesn't step down from a verbal fight or a duel so he is very annoying to play against and very nice to have in your team.'

Nominated for the Bundesliga's Rookie of the Month award at the end of September, Bellingham's opponents were already resorting to elaborate and ultimately unsuccessful methods to stop him. While Bellingham was still only a couple of months past his 17th birthday, fellow nominee Silas Wamangituka Fundu was a relatively experienced player at 21. Or at least that was the official story at the time. Later that season, Stuttgart were forced to release a statement declaring that not only was their Congolese winger a year older than had previously been claimed, but that his real name was actually Silas Katompa Mvumpa. The player was fined €30,000 and banned for three months by the DFB. Completing the shortlist of three was Armenia Bielefeld's Amos Pieper, a legitimate contender who had started out in Dortmund's academy before moving east. A strong central defender, Pieper would form part of the side that would claim the European under-21 championship with Germany at the end of the campaign.

The adjudicators in these awards tend to favour attackers over defenders, but in this case they went for the exciting middle ground in choosing the dynamic young English midfielder who'd dropped into the league over the summer. Old Silas can console himself with the fact that on top of the aforementioned sanctions, missing out on the accolade at least meant he was spared the additional embarrassment of handing back his prize.

Jude was enjoying himself but his debut goal was not the prelude to a deluge. Almost seven months would pass between his first and second goals for Dortmund, but that was no reliable gauge for the education he was receiving in his new environment. On 20 October he made his European debut in a Champions League match away to Lazio in Rome. Marshalled by the experienced Lucas Leiva in midfield, the Italian side were much too savvy for Dortmund and quickly assembled a two-goal lead. As Favre regrouped at half-time, Jude was substituted in favour of Reyna. It was a sore lesson, one that hurt, but he learned quickly, bouncing back to play in all six matches as Dortmund qualified for the knockout stage as group winners from a section that also included Zenit St Petersburg and Club Brugge.

'He was more focused on defensive duties at the beginning,' says Müller. 'But right from the start you could see that this was just not enough for him. Everybody could see that Borussia Dortmund had a high-class talent, someone who was developing rapidly. I remember he once said that the style was different to what he was used to in the English Championship. The teams in Germany are always very offensive so he always had space to show his skills.'

No side that boasts Erling Braut Haaland should need worry too much about goals, but Favre was not managing to coax the best out of the talented group of players at his disposal. After losing 5-1 to Stuttgart in December, he was removed and assistant coach Edin Terzić installed in his place. Born in West Germany to Bosnian and Croatian parents, Terzić was raised locally and had been a journeyman forward in the German lower leagues, obtaining a degree in sports science along the way. He took on a scouting role at Dortmund aged 27, reporting directly to first-team manager Jürgen Klopp and went on to work with Slaven Bilić who took him to Beşiktaş and West Ham United as an assistant. He'd returned to Dortmund in 2018 to join the newly installed Favre and was considered an invigorating choice to step in by Dortmund's chief executive. 'He took over the team when it was half dead and brought it to life,' Hans-Joachim Watzke would later remark.

Dortmund rallied to such an extent that they reached the quarter-finals of the Champions League and went on to lift the German Cup, the DFB-Pokal. Haaland was the headliner, with Marco Reus, Sancho and Bellingham providing an able support cast as Terzić encouraged the team to express itself. After beating Sevilla in the first knock-out round of the Champions League, Dortmund were drawn against Manchester City, giving Jude the chance to return to English soil. City would win 4-2 on aggregate, but a Bellingham goal in the second leg in Germany had temporarily levelled the tie – and made him the youngest Englishman to score in the competition. 'Not bad for a Championship player,' he remarked when asked how he felt his first crack at Europe had gone.

His fourth and final goal of the season arrived in the cup semi-final rout of Holstein Kiel and he was chosen to start the final against RB Leipzig in Berlin's Olympic Stadium. There, on a stage once illuminated by Jesse Owens, Dortmund ran over the top of their opponents with Sancho and Haaland scoring twice apiece in a dismantling of Julian Nagelsmann's XI. The players cavorted with their trophy but, with no supporters in this vast arena, it felt like no way for any player to celebrate a major win, far less a 17-year-old who was tasting victory for the first time. The cup win showcased the raw talent of Dortmund but consistency remained an issue. Leipzig actually nudged Terzić's side into third place in the Bundesliga's final standings, while both teams trailed champions Bayern Munich by double digits at the final count.

For Jude the close season saw a shift in focus. Handed his full international debut by Gareth Southgate in the March friendly against the Republic of Ireland, he was awarded a place in the squad for the Euro 2020 finals, which had been pushed back a year by the pandemic. Among the many extra rules and mitigations put in place for the tournament by UEFA was an extension in squad size by three places. Even without that wiggle room, Southgate might well have picked the teenager on form alone. The Euros adventure would see Jude make three substitute appearances and experience the thrill and the pressure of a run to the final of a major tournament.

When he returned to Germany it was to a new manager, namely Marco Rose who had been recruited from Borussia Mönchengladbach with Dortmund finding a new role for Terzić as technical director. Also of Croatian descent and a former university student of psychology, Rose's assistant René Marić had plenty in common with Terzić and was instantly captivated with a player who had only just turned 18. 'Everyone was in awe of Jude and immediately I understood why,' said Marić. 'That mix of age, quality, but also that presence, leadership and maturity. With Jude the things you can work with him on are on a different level. First the way he can turn under pressure, solve situations and he can go one against one which is rare for a central midfielder. Creatively be a dribbler and a passer. That's what separates him from most box-to-box midfielders at that age. If he really fulfils his potential in big spaces he can be like a Steven Gerrard, looking to score but also defend in his own box and do everything in between. But also in small spaces he can be like Zidane. To turn around opponents and find a solution under high pressure. He has that very unique mix. I think he is just going to be a superstar.'

In October, Jude scored a quite exquisite goal away to Arminia Bielefeld. First shaping to shoot as he received the ball 20 yards out, the Dortmund midfielder would not actually pull the trigger until he'd dribbled past three players.

The first was taken out by a trademark chop with his right foot and then it was into slalom mode as his revolving hips took him inside and out of two more before a dinked left-foot finish over the goalkeeper. It was as good an individual strike as you'll see and rightly earned him the Bundesliga Goal of the Month award. The goal showcased the best of Bellingham, but while his dancing feet continued to draw acclaim, his mouth suddenly let him down.

As helpful as the media training back at Birmingham had been, the mock interview situations staged in a quiet room back at the Wast Hills training complex in the Midlands could only prepare him so far. When Dortmund met Bayern Munich at the Westfalenstadion on 4 December, they trailed by a single point and sensed an opportunity to claim top spot. The match that played out was tense, fiery and exciting. It eventually spun in Bayern's favour when Robert Lewandowski claimed the odd goal in five. The game ended in acrimony with Rose – booked earlier for protesting the non-award of a Dortmund penalty – shown a red card by referee Felix Zwayer. Handed a microphone by pitchside reporter Jan Aage Fjørtoft, and placed in front of a television camera in the immediate aftermath, Bellingham turned his own fire on the official, who'd awarded Bayern's penalty for a disputed handball offence by Mats Hummels in the final quarter of an hour. Himself booked during the match, Bellingham questioned not only the handball decision but the very appointment of the official, saying: 'Well, for me it wasn't. It hits him (Hummels) but I don't even think he's looking at the ball. You can look at a lot of the decisions in the game. You give a referee that's match-fixed before, the biggest game in Germany, what do you expect?'

Bellingham's comments were a direct reference to a six-month ban issued to Zwayer in 2005 following his role in a match-fixing scandal. A linesman at the time, Zwayer had been drawn into a wider plot centred on referee Robert Hoyzer, who was found guilty of accepting bribes to fix several matches. Zwayer was himself found to have accepted a single bribe for a match in which Hoyzer had officiated, but a Munich judge ruled that he had made no deliberate errors in the game and had also provided evidence to help convict Hoyzer. In the 16 years hence, Zwayer had carefully rebuilt his reputation, but Bellingham's words created a furore. Zwayer would not be seen again for two months and the German FA acted swiftly. Bellingham was fined €40,000 by the DFB and warned as to his future conduct.

The next day, Zwayer gave an interview to *Bild*, saying: 'For me it's not about punishment, but about the realisation that he went too far. I would accept a sincere apology. The statement deliberately creates the false impression that I did not referee the match to the best of my ability. It is personal, disparaging and disrespectful. Even if you put yourself in the subjective perspective, which is marked by emotion, his statement is far from professional or factual.'

As we'll discuss later, this was not the last occasion on which Bellingham and Zwayer would meet in high-profile circumstances. It wasn't just officialdom that was starting to feel the spikier side of Jude's personality. Teammates too were finding that he had little patience for those not adhering to his own high standards of performance. Most famously there was a Europa League match-up against Rangers. With Haaland out injured, Dortmund did not go into the match in great fettle and found themselves three goals down after just 49 minutes. A left-foot raker from Bellingham pulled them back into the contest but a 2-4 defeat made the ensuing trip to Glasgow a stiff proposition. On the pitch, Bellingham had been Dortmund's main driving force and, off it, having served some time out of the spotlight following the Zwayer flashpoint, he retook responsibility in front of the cameras too. 'There's a bit of hope because there's the second leg and there's not one person in the changing room that's going to give up,' he said. 'And I won't let them. We are going to go there and give everything. Personally I can't wait to play at Ibrox; it's one of the best stadiums in Europe in my opinion when it's packed on a European night.'

'I won't let them.' Coming from a Mats Hummels or a Marco Reus, no one would have batted an eyelid. But in the context of the natural hierarchy of a dressing room you could imagine Rose being both thrilled by the mettle of the now 18-year-old midfielder and wary of the danger that such words might sow disharmony. He backed up his words by again scoring at Ibrox, but with the game poised at 2-2 on the night and Rangers still two goals to the good on aggregate, he quite visibly and audibly lost his cool in the Glasgow cauldron, reacting to a misplaced pass from Nicolas Schulz and berating his teammate for the error with the scream: 'You're fucking shit.'

Dortmund had only ended up in a match-up with the Scots after a flaky Champions League performance in which they missed out on progression to the knockout stage on head-to-head goal difference to Sporting Lisbon. Bellingham had again looked at home on the elite stage scoring in the victories over Beşiktaş and Sporting before three straight defeats left Rose's side well adrift of runaway section leaders Ajax.

'There was a running discussion, especially among us journalists, saying this Dortmund team was lacking the personalities to be a leader,' observes Müller. 'In his second season you could see that there was now a leader, and his name was Jude Bellingham. Some said this was not healthy because he was so young, maybe the youngest player, and he was the one standing up on the pitch. But you could see already the way he communicated with his teammates, he pushed them. He also had a little aggressive touch in his style and his character of playing, maybe a bit too aggressive in the way he sometimes communicated with his teammates.

'The crowd, and this is always very important in Dortmund, loved him right from the start. Not so much because of his skills which were already great, but especially because of his attitude. He never gave up. This is something that is honoured by the fans of Borussia Dortmund, who have a different approach compared to Bayern Munich. The fans of Bayern want to see good football, fine football and successful football. But the fans of Dortmund want to see emotional, aggressive football and Jude fitted in perfectly. For Nico Schulz in that certain situation I could imagine those words were not very nice to hear. And there were also situations during those coronavirus games, without any supporters when you could hear everything that was being said on the pitch. The way Jude would yell at his teammates reminded me of lower-class football games where the language is a little bit ruder in certain situations. He was once confronted with that question and he said that yes, he had been to a lot of non-league games to watch his father Mark Bellingham and of course he heard all of this trash talk.'

Jude was enjoying a first-class football education, but there had been a glaring deficiency in the experience. Even deep into his second year at the club, Covid restrictions were limiting the number of spectators at games and, like a number of teams whose football benefits from a synergy with a supportive crowd, Dortmund never quite seemed to be equal to the sum of their parts. Paul Lambert knows what it's like to gain the adulation of the Dortmund's South Bank, alongside Liverpool's now seated Kop, perhaps the most famous section of terracing in the sporting world and one that looms like a ski slope behind the goal at the Westfalen, accommodating more than 24,000 fans at capacity. For Lambert, the support of the Yellow Wall is inextricably linked to the memories he made in Germany. Signed on a Bosman in the summer of 1996, he was a BVB player for little over a year, but made an indelible mark, something he attributes to his wholehearted yet understated approach to the game.

Lambert recalls: 'The fans wouldn't have known me from Adam because I was coming from Motherwell on a Bosman but, just by pure chance, I got in the team. We played Düsseldorf at home on the second night of the season and I had one of those games where everything went right. I set up a couple of goals and all of a sudden the crowd started to sing my name. I'll never forget this: Paulo Sousa and Karl-Heinz Riedle were coming off the bench and I started to slowly walk over and looked up and saw that it wasn't my number. That's when the penny dropped. I wasn't coming out of this team. I was a mainstay. The crowd just seemed to love the way I played, the never-say-die attitude or whatever. If you can relate to the fans and what they go through, they'll love that, but I think you've got to be humble too. All the world-class players I've played against have that humility. Gheorghe Hagi. Top bloke. Zinedine Zidane. Top bloke.

'When I first met Jude he had his mum with him. I said: "He's doing great." Turned to Jude and said: "Keep those feet on the ground." Denise said: "You listen to that advice!" So he has that family grounding which is important. Being from Glasgow I could relate to Dortmund. The working city. You go out to warm up and that yellow wall can be full. They used to sing for me and our wing-back Jörg Heinrich together: "Paul Lambert, Jörg Heinrich, Paul Lambert, Jörg Heinrich." So it became a custom that we'd go and wave and they'd move on to Mathias Sammer or whoever. That wall is like a magnet. When you shoot towards that end you think you're unbeatable. It drives you on and on. It's incredible.'

It was soon after that defeat to Rangers that Bellingham was properly introduced to Lambert, who's continued to visit Dortmund regularly since leaving the club for Celtic back in 1997. He'd been a key performer in the club's historic Champions League win over Juventus, performing doggedly to subdue Zidane and also producing a moment of creative class, slinging over the cross from which Karl-Heinz Riedle opened the scoring in a 3-1 victory. That night earned him a permanent place in Dortmund folklore and so it was only natural that Jude might be drawn to the Scot's story – even if a later chapter saw him manage Birmingham's great city rivals Aston Villa.

'I'd first seen Jude at Birmingham and thought the kid could really play,' says Lambert. 'We actually met at the training ground in Dortmund and he asked me for a picture which we did just outside the training ground. I watched him training on that first visit and thought he was a proper player, training the way he plays, on it all the time. Same with Haaland, the way the two of them operated in training was at another level. Haaland never missed; in front of goal it's like he's taking sweets. A while later I went back over to watch a game and told him I was coming. I texted him and said I'd be in the lounge afterwards and we could maybe say hello. He texted back and said: "Hi, Paul, which floor are you on? Not sure if you're a collector but I've got my game shirt for you." 'He gave me the shirt and it was soaking wet. I said: "Jude, can I give you a word of advice? Great players don't sweat and that jersey is soaking!" We had to take it back to the hotel and dry it off to get it in my bag.'

The two have remained close. Lambert proudly shows a text message received from Jude a few months earlier. It's a screenshot of a BVB birthday message posted online in his honour. Underneath a picture of Lambert holding the Champions League trophy aloft, Jude has attached the word 'legend'. The appreciation is mutual. 'I think if you asked Jude Bellingham to go and play right-back he could do it,' adds Lambert. 'Like all top players he knows where to be on the pitch – he doesn't need a manager to tell him. Game intelligence is huge and Jude has that in abundance. Even on that first visit, I had a feeling Madrid would be the perfect fit for him. We've seen him play much further forward since he went to Spain, always hitting the box waiting for those cutbacks, but in Dortmund he was more a conventional midfielder. He has the athleticism to keep going up and down the pitch and he is bloody good with both feet.'

Jude's second season had ended in another second-placed finish and there was already a very definite sense that he might be starting to outgrow his environment. Physically he had broadened out and the added power in his game made him an irrepressible force in the middle of the park. Not only was he included in the Bundesliga team of the season but, later that year, he was named runner-up to Barcelona's Pedri in the Kopa Trophy, the annual award presented to the world's best player under the age of 21. Capped at senior level by England, Jude was now a truly international talent and one prized by all the big clubs in Europe. Already Madrid were in motion with chief scout Juni Calafat and chief executive José Ángel Sánchez eyeing another big emerging talent.

Dortmund's ultimate plan to trade at a profit would facilitate Madrid's plan, but first they had another big asset to sell. Ahead of Jude's third and final year in Germany, BVB sold Haaland to Manchester City for £51 million, the value of the release clause inserted in his contract when he moved from Austria. With 86 goals in 89 appearances, Haaland had scored at a phenomenal rate and the loss of such a rampant, deadly finisher left a void in the Dortmund team as they regrouped for another tilt at toppling Bayern.

The club hierarchy had already twisted again on the managerial front, sacking Rose and replacing him with Terzić, this time on a permanent contract to 2025. Although apparently weakened further by the sale of

Swiss defender Manuel Akanji, who followed Haaland to Manchester City, Dortmund actually improved. Terzić was obviously responsible but the role of the No. 22 should not be understated. A sign of the faith he placed in the midfielder lay in the decision to appoint him to the squad's leadership council as third captain behind Reus and vice skipper Hummels. In the absence of Haaland, Terzić did not pin his hopes on a single striker and was rewarded by a spread of goals. In the end it was his teenage midfielder who ended up as top scorer.

Bellingham's appetite was evident on the opening day of the new campaign when he struck in the cup match against 1860 Munich. It would take him a few weeks to find his rhythm but the Champions League again proved to be his stage and he scored in four consecutive group matches against Copenhagen, Manchester City and Sevilla (twice). By the time the season broke in mid-November for the 2022 World Cup, he had registered nine goals in all competitions and, chosen to start the opening match against Iran, he hit double figures with the first of England's tournament goals in Qatar.

In the new year, Dortmund retreated to a mid-winter camp in Marbella to recharge ahead of the second half of the season. Towards the end of the camp it's customary for the BVB players to join travelling supporters at a designated venue and mix socially. 'I remember Jude Bellingham came over and he really took his time to talk to the supporters and listen to their problems,' says Müller, who was there in his professional capacity. 'Some were telling him about the trouble they had trying to follow the team abroad and he really listened to them. I'm not sure if he understood

Welcome home: Video footage of Jude Bellingham accepting the celebrated No.5 shirt from Real Madrid president Florentino Pérez is played to the assembled media before a press conference to mark his official unveiling (PA Images / Alamy Stock Photo)

A new hero: The 20-year-old recruit celebrates his debut goal against Athletic Bilbao, announcing his arrival as a player with shoulders broad enough to carry the weight of expectation (Independent Photo Agency / Alamy Stock Photo)

Team Bellingham: Proud parents Denise and Mark with brothers Jude and Jobe, pictured at the BBC Sports Personality of the Year Awards in 2021, have created a formidable family unit that has nurtured the talent and personality of two rising stars
(PA Images / Alamy Stock Photo)

Where it all began: Jude, in the No.22 that would later be retired in his honour, celebrates in front of the adoring Birmingham City supporters after scoring against Stoke City at St Andrew's in 2019 (PA Images / Alamy Stock Photo)

Heir apparent: Going head to head with Wayne Rooney, then a veteran with Derby County in 2020, was symbolic for a player who would carry the same talismanic status for his country. It was Rooney's name that Jude had chosen to adorn his first England kit as a young fan and the pair were opponents in his final game for Birmingham.
(PA Images/ Alamy Stock Photo)

Spanning the generations: The mural depicting Trevor Francis and Jude Bellingham on the side of the Birmingham City club shop provides a lasting reminder of the star men
(Graeme Croser)

Humble beginnings: Currywurst and pommes frites is the house special at Lotte's Curry emporium, the new name for the birthplace of Borussia Dortmund (Graeme Croser)

First of many: Jude and fellow Englishman Jadon Sancho celebrate Dortmund's 4–0 cup final rout against RB Leipzig in the 2021 showdown – his first, but not last, taste of trophy success (DPA Picture Alliance/ Alamy Stock Photo)

Man in the middle: Jude, in the DFB Cup final against RB Leipzig at the Olympic Stadium in Berlin in 2021, making a trademark run from midfield. He was an instant hit in German football after his switch from boyhood team Birmingham

(DPA Picture Alliance / Alamy Stock Photo)

Above. A club of scale: The Santiago Bernabéu stands as a monument to Madrid's great past and beacon of a bright future, after an 800 million Euro development project (Graeme Croser)

Right. Underground movement: Madrid fans, resplendent in Bellingham shirts, flock to the stadium from the nearby metro station to see their hero (Graeme Croser)

Global appeal: Londoner Shaun Singh and Venezuelan fan Samuel Millan are among the Madridistas who have chosen Bellingham to adorn their kits (Graeme Croser)

The big prize: Jude celebrates victory against his old team Borussia Dortmund in the 2024 Champions League final at Wembley, with an assist in the 2-0 win adding to his incredible contribution in a debut season to remember (DPA Picture Alliance / Alamy Stock Photo)

The man, the moment: A stunning overhead kick equaliser against Slovakia in the last 16 of Euro 2024 kept England's dream alive (Associated Press / Alamy Stock Photo)

Who else? Jude celebrates his dramatic strike – with elation, relief and defiance crashing together. The experience of another major tournament provided another building block in a career that is only just beginning (DPA Picture Alliance / Alamy Stock Photo) absolutely everything but he was very patient and he was the last of the players to leave the pub on this particular night. It was quite impressive.'

Dortmund entertained Augsburg in the first game after the restart and it was Bellingham who opened the scoring in a 4-3 win. Arne Engels was entitled to feel he had done a textbook job of squeezing the space in front of his opponent, but Bellingham's stepover and shift of the ball was imperceptibly quick, the finish devastating. It was the start of a seven-game winning run that announced Dortmund's status as bona fide title challengers and, in the circumstances, a Champions League exit to Chelsea felt like no disaster. A 6-1 victory over Köln showcased the power of Terzić's side and, although Bellingham was not scoring freely, he was playing with verve and purpose, clearly revelling in the pursuit of a big prize.

By the time the next showdown with Bayern rolled round it was Dortmund who sat top and Bayern reacted with indignation. Less than two years earlier they had paid a world-record sum of €25 million to prise their coach Julian Nagelsmann away from RB Leipzig, but the fear of losing their title prompted them to abandon their investment. Thomas Tuchel, an ex-Dortmund coach, was the man appointed and he drew a devastating response from the Bayern players who smelled blood from the moment Dortmund keeper Gregor Kobel kicked fresh air and allowed Dayot Upamecano's long clearance to trundle over the line. Two more from Thomas Müller effectively ended the contest by half-time and Kingsley Coman added a fourth before two late, academic Dortmund counters made the result less embarrassing.

Knocked out of the German Cup in midweek by Leipzig, the potential was there for Dortmund's season to fall apart, but Terzić rallied his group and urged them to summon one final push for the line. Bellingham proved up for the fight and found his shooting boots again, netting four times in six games as Dortmund pushed Bayern down the home straight.

Yet there was trouble in store. A knee problem ruled Bellingham out of the penultimate game of the campaign, a 3-0 win at Augsburg, and had not cleared up in time for him to face Mainz on the final day. Back on top after Bayern's surprise slip-up at home to Leipzig, Dortmund were two points ahead and now needed only to beat mid-table Mainz at home to guarantee their first Meisterschale trophy since 2012. Bellingham was not fit to take part but, presumably for psychological reasons, Terzić named him among the substitutes anyway. It had no positive effect. Dortmund shrivelled under the pressure and fell two goals behind inside 24 minutes, with Sébastien Haller missing a penalty in between. Bayern were handling the strain a little better but were themselves forced into panic when Kingsley Coman's early goal was cancelled out in the 81st minute. And so, even as Dortmund trailed 2-1 in the final minutes, the title was still, somehow, almost theirs. As Dortmund fans anxiously checked their phones for updates from Köln, news of a late Musiala winner filtered through to depress what was now a Wailing Wall. Niklas Süle's equaliser for 2-2 deep in stoppage time was ultimately an irrelevance.

Unused in the game, Bellingham was inconsolable at the end. Terzić, the man who'd done so much to help accelerate his development, tried anyway. 'Terzić's approach towards

Jude Bellingham was different from the other coaches at Dortmund,' explains Müller. 'Favre was an elderly coach who didn't relate in the same way and Marco Rose also had a more distant approach to the players. Terzić is an emotional coach so he was really close to him.'

Once again Bellingham was named in the team of the year and he was also crowned the Bundesliga's player of the year by his fellow pros. But he was hungry for something more. Madrid were waiting and despite their troubles in the previous year, Carlo Ancelotti and his players were a proven winning machine. 'The only disappointment of Jude's stay in Germany was that he did not get the chance to have a proper celebration,' continues Müller. 'The cup win in 2021 was like a ghost game with no supporters; the whole atmosphere had nothing to do with the football we all love. When Dortmund wins a title it is something extraordinary and they have one of the biggest parties in Germany, maybe 500,000 people on the streets. He was really sad that he could not say goodbye with the trophy and I guess it was even worse because he was not able to play on the last day. I am pretty sure it's impossible to find any supporter of Dortmund who speaks badly of him. Of course they had some hope that maybe he would stay another year, but they understood his decision to leave.'

Lambert sympathises. Although he stayed for less than half of the three-year time span served by Jude, he achieved immortal status and, before his mid-season departure to Celtic, was given a tear-jerking farewell from the Yellow Wall. 'I had to stand in front of that wall myself. It was too much. I was crying. It's a shame Jude didn't get that kind of send-off.'

Chapter 8

A POR LA 15

AT DORTMUND, Bellingham learned to play for a club of scale, one that continues to revere the side which reached the pinnacle and became champions of Europe in 1997. The names of Möller, Riedle, Lambert and Heinrich are forever legends at the Westfalen Stadion and images of each are venerated in commemoration of the club's single greatest achievement. At Madrid the expectations are significantly greater. When Jude checked in he was pictured alongside the club's proud president Florentino Pérez in front of a row of 14 European Cups. There are separate walls in the trophy chambers for the remaining European titles. Another for the domestic baubles. And a cabinet for all the Ballon d'Or trophies.

Yes, success in a Spanish context is important. But perhaps less so than in the days when a La Liga title was the only ticket towards participation in the European Cup. The pressure to perform at the very pinnacle of the continental game is one felt keenly in the manager's office. 'The identity of this club is the Champions League,' says Davide Ancelotti. 'Go to the training ground and you'll see no photos of the teams that have won La Liga. Only the

Champions League. So the goal here is clear. In terms of the club's DNA, the Champions League is the most important thing. You can't win it every year of course. But you have to compete for it.'

The popular image of Don Carlo Ancelotti is of the relaxed chief, immaculate in his designer suit, conducting himself with a grace that sees him float above the pressures of elite level management. But entering the 2023–24 season, there was a weight on his shoulders. As his son states, there is never a guarantee of coming out on top of the pile in club football's most prestigious competition. But at Madrid there is a way to fail.

Real's loss to Manchester City in the previous year was not easily swallowed by Pérez's hierarchy. After a draw in the first leg, Pep Guardiola presided over the complete suffocation of Madrid in Manchester. The four-goal margin of victory was at least as much as City deserved and would have been more without a strong evening's work from goalkeeper Thibaut Courtois. City would go on to lift the trophy with a win over Inter Milan in Istanbul, a moment Guardiola had grafted seven years to achieve and the City fans had waited a lifetime to see. Yet what is regarded as a dream elsewhere is akin to a birthright in the palace of Madrid, where the legends of Di Stéfano and Puskás set the standard.

It's instructive to wander the trophy room on the stadium tour of the Bernabéu and consider the sheer magnitude of the club's success. In the first five seasons following the European Cup's inception in 1955 there was only one name on the trophy, and it was in this era that those white jerseys acquired an aura that spread across not only the continent but the globe. As Jude Bellingham was paraded as a Madrid player in June 2023, perhaps the most arresting image of the day was of the young player standing in front of those 14 trophies, that number double the haul of AC Milan, the most successful of the remaining multiple winners.

Against that backdrop it was imperative that Ancelotti's team make a strong start in the following season's edition or the Italian would face a graver inquisition. Not always the quickest starters in the competition, Madrid left it late to claim victory in their opening group fixture against Union Berlin and, in the thick of his scoring streak, it was Jude who provided the killer moment, spinning 360 degrees to knock in Federico Valverde's parried shot deep in stoppage time. He made it two in two with a fine solo effort in Naples but here the hyperbole really started to ramp up. The choice of shirt number had made comparisons with Zidane inevitable, but the name of Di Stéfano was also being invoked by commentators eager not to be left trailing the hype train. And when this latest goal hit the net in the Diego Armando Maradona Stadium, you can guess what happened next.

'That's a bit too much,' reasoned the match-winner when hit with the Maradona link. 'From what I've seen on YouTube and documentaries, his quality was a bit more than mine – or a lot more. I'm just trying to contribute in a Jude way.' Even the normally sober BBC hailed the goal as a possible winner of the Puskás Award, the annual bauble doled out for the best goal scored in world football across all levels and genders. In truth, the strike probably wouldn't have made Jude's top three for the season, yet his was now officially a worldwide bandwagon and there was no shortage of people trying to clamber aboard.

Jude maintained his scoring record with the winner away to Braga on match night three, calmly placing the ball into the bottom corner from the edge of the box. Ancelotti rested him for the return against the Portuguese but he was back for match night five, steering home David Alaba's cross to maintain his strike rate with a fourth in four games against Napoli, helping the team to a 4-2 win that ensured top spot in the group. Madrid got the maximum 18-point mark by winning on their return to Germany, defeating Union Berlin in an entertaining closer to the Group C schedule. Union had ceded proper home advantage for their first foray into the competition by locating away from their compact and unique woodland Alten Försterei home to the Olympic Stadium, which can accommodate more than double the number of spectators. The Union fans did their best to make it loud and noisy for Madrid and the players held up their end of the bargain, too, taking the lead just before half-time and pegging their visitors back after Joselu had struck twice in the second half. Dani Ceballos conjured a winner late in the match on the back of a Bellingham assist, a contribution that ensured his return to Germany had ended successfully.

This was his fourth campaign of European football and his contribution to Madrid's utter dominance of the section helped secure and consolidate Ancelotti's position. If the previous season's exit hadn't quite been put to bed, the club were sufficiently convinced by Ancelotti's restorative work and his ingenuity in solving the post-Benzema conundrum that they awarded him with a new contract. The Italian could approach the knockout stages emboldened.

Before then, Madrid were flown to another continent to

contest the Spanish Super Cup in Saudi Arabia, an event that is a faintly ridiculous manifestation of the commercial pressures that are constantly finding new angles to exploit the sport. Originally conceived as a two-legged tie between the La Liga and Copa del Rey winners, the event was expanded to a four-team format in 2019 when the Saudis came calling with a contract worth an estimated €40 million annually to the Spanish Football Federation. As cup holders, Real received an invite alongside league champions Barcelona with Osasuna and Atlético Madrid making up the quartet as nearest challengers for the two titles. The four teams stood to share half of the spoils, with the prize money weighted on an invitation basis to the two trophy holders. As for the trivialities of the football, Madrid faced off against Atlético in their semi-final and clinched a place in the final courtesy of extra-time goals from Joselu and Brahim Díaz after the 90 minutes finished in a 3-3 draw. If there was any residual tiredness it did not show in a final that was effectively finished by half-time thanks to Vinicius Jr's quick-fire hat-trick. Quite unusually, Jude had not contributed any of the nine goals scored by Madrid over the two games in Riyadh, but did provide a lovely assist for Vinicius's first in the final. It was hardly the most important night in his football career, yet alongside the very distinct sense of powerful momentum, there was a feeling of achievement as he clutched his first winner's medal for his new club.

Any thoughts of a perfect first year in Spain were extinguished by defeat to Atlético in the Copa del Rey in the very next game, but the great priority was looming back into view, with a last 16 tie setting up another journey to Germany – and a reunion with his former Dortmund coach Marco Rose, now in charge at RB Leipzig. Forced off with an ankle injury after scoring twice against Girona at the weekend, Jude was ruled out of the first leg and was scarcely in better fettle by the time the second leg rolled round in late February. After three games out he'd returned to face Valencia but was red-carded at the end after furiously protesting the officials' decision to disallow what would have been a last-minute winning goal.

Despite that indiscretion he was needed for the second leg against Leipzig. His replacement Brahim Díaz had secured a 1-0 lead going into the return, but with Spanish playmaker Dani Olmo pulling the strings, Leipzig remained a live threat even after Jude's surging run ended with an assist for Vinicius Jr to open the scoring. A Leipzig equaliser kept the tie tense to the end and sharpened the impression any further gains in the competition would be hard won.

Ancelotti may well have winced when the draw for the quarter-finals threw up a rematch with City. Madrid might be going well and City not quite as self-assured domestically, but had the gap between the teams narrowed sufficiently since their last one-sided meeting? The question might have unnerved either side and provoked a cagey, tentative opening to the tie. Not these coaches. Not these sets of players. The Madridistas can only have feared the worst when, with less than two minutes on the clock, Bernardo Silva gave City the lead with a free-kick that really ought to have been stopped by Andriy Lunin. Ten minutes later the pendulum had swung – a Camavinga shot deflected in off Rúben Dias and then Rodrygo squeezed a finish in past

Emerson. If those three goals were untidy, the second half was an exhibition of shooting. Phil Foden arrowed one into the top corner before Joško Gvardiol scored his first City goal from outside the box. Best of all was the Valverde volley that exploded off the Uruguayan's right foot for a 3-3 finish.

And so, on to England. Madrid's comms department, who had previously been careful to minimise Bellingham's appearances in front of the media, decided to put him forward for the pre-match press conference ahead of the second leg in Manchester. When word got out, journalists jostled for elbow room. In front of this packed audience, the 20-year-old was in dazzling, authoritative form, answering squarely and meeting each inquisitor with sympathetic eye contact. There were words of respect for City but the overwhelming theme was a glowing testimony of the Ancelotti effect on his development. He said: 'The sign of a good manager is when he can make you believe you are a bit better than you think you were before. He fills me with that confidence every day. He gives me the freedom to roam the pitch and be as effective as possible. Not only that he is a top person and he makes me feel comfortable. Obviously it was a big move for me coming here with so many massive characters and big legends, but he has been amazing in helping me adapt and understand my own potential. It's the first time I have played more as a ten. At Dortmund I was playing a lot deeper. And at Birmingham all over the place. It's definitely down to him why I have had the start at Madrid and I am very grateful for everything he has done for me so far.'

The second leg did not play out with quite the same abandon, but there was a moment of Bellingham magic as he pulled Dani Carvajal's clearance out of the sky and worked the space in which Valverde and Vinicius were able to combine and supply Rodrygo for the Real goal. A Kevin De Bruyne equaliser ensured the tie went the distance and, eventually, to penalties. As the players collected themselves before the game's ultimate test of nerve and precision, a familiar anthem sounded over the Etihad's speakers, one that, perhaps unwittingly, united both sets of supporters. Despite the rivalry between England's powerhouse north-western cities, City have adopted a tune by Liverpool's favourite band and the pocket of Madridistas in the corner were delighted to join in by bellowing the chorus of 'Hey Jude' in the direction of their No. 5.

Once under way, the shootout placed Bellingham second on the Madrid order. Top spot went to the wily, experienced Luka Modrić. Ancelotti couldn't have wished for a surer opener, but something unusual happened in the run-up. Few would regard the Etihad as one of the game's great cauldrons, but as the magnitude of the moment blazed into focus, the atmosphere thickened in a cacophony of boos and jeers that soundtracked the Croatian's walk towards the spot. With Julián Alvarez having tucked away the first against a much gentler backdrop, Modrić's face betrayed a degree of strain as he set himself for the run-up. Whether Ederson could tell from 18 yards range was moot as he sprung right in a pre-determined move to scoop away the kick. Modrić's subsequent, wild lash at the rebound was out of character yet his loss of composure was arguably the decisive moment in the shoot-out. His frustration sent the ball looping high behind the goal where an opportunistic City fan decided to hang on to a souvenir before eventually being shamed into bouncing it back down off the upper tier. The delay was sufficient enough to cause the next taker, Bernardo Silva, to second-guess himself and fluff his penalty timidly into the arms of Lunin. The misstep dulled the edge off the crowd, but Bellingham strode forward like it wouldn't have mattered anyway. The run-up, including a little stutter to disguise his intentions, ended with a calm, rolled finish into the bottom corner. Real had parity and the psychological advantage which they pressed home to take their place in the last four.

After some unbridled celebrations in a squad huddle, Bellingham broke free to lead the charge to the away support. Within minutes he had a microphone in his hand and was recounting his thoughts to broadcasters TNT's pitch-side panel. 'It's relief,' he sighed. 'I have played against City before and you have to work really hard to beat them. I was pretty much dead on my feet at the end so to win the game was a big reward.'

Although he was now an experienced international with two major tournaments under his belt, the opportunity to hear Bellingham speak was something of a novelty for English television viewers. While it would be wrong to say his progress on the continent had been ignored by the country's media, a combination of factors pushed his exploits towards the fringes of football coverage. The hyper-focus on the all-important Premier League was one issue, geography another, not least when the Covid travel restrictions were in place. Finally there was the protective collaboration between the family and his clubs to minimise his exposure. Hearing and seeing him speak so lucidly came over as a revelation.

'I could never have dreamed of how well it has gone,' he said of his opening season in Spain. 'Not just because of the performances and the goals but just the feeling you get playing for the club. You get to put that badge on the chest and you are just so grateful to be there. Our biggest strength is that he (Ancelotti) finds a way to let a lot of the boys play with freedom. Other teams are a bit more structured in terms of their passing styles and their patterns of play, but one of our biggest strengths is that we are so off the cuff. As a man he fills you with calmness and confidence. Before the game there I caught him yawning. I said to him, "Boss, are you tired?" And he said, "Yeah, you need to go and excite me!"'

Visibly impressed by what he was listening to, former Manchester United and England defender Rio Ferdinand asked if the badge weighed heavily because of all the star names that have played for Real: 'I think you have got to see it as responsibility and not pressure,' replied Jude. 'You have to be willing to be criticised, be under that scrutiny and that spotlight. The club do a great job and they ease you in if they don't think you are ready. But if you are here it means you can handle it so you have just got to trust the process.'

Into the semis and yet another trip to Germany awaited. El Clásico stands as one of the truly great domestic rivalries in world football, yet Madrid have also developed a continental equivalent down the years. Among all the cross-border rivalries in Europe, there's none quite as intensely practised as the enmity that exists between Real Madrid and Bayern Munich. Call it Der Clásico. Or El Klassiker. Down the decades these clubs have sparred ferociously in European competitions, but quite bizarrely have never met in a final.

That record remained intact, but the feeling around this last-four encounter felt as big as any one-off final.

As ever, Don Carlo Ancelotti managed to float calmly above the madness even if he had a couple of his own bones to pick with the powerhouse of German football. He'd lifted the Bundesliga title during his one full season at Bayern before being removed from his position after a poor start to the ensuing Champions League campaign. And when Madrid turned to Bellingham and the future when they made their marquee signing in the summer of 2023, it was Bayern who swooped in to land Ancelotti's preferred choice of striker, investing very much in the present when they prised Harry Kane away from Tottenham for a similar fee. The match-up between the current England captain and his heir apparent was the most obvious subplot to the semi-final, but the presence of Jamal Musiala in the Germans' ranks provided a more relevant comparison. Musiala (nine months older) and Bellingham were capped alongside each other at youth level for England and have remained close as their respective career journeys took them to the Bundesliga. Bellingham may have embraced his Dortmund challenge wholeheartedly, but Musiala took things a stage further after he switched from Chelsea to Bayern in 2019. Even by the time of that move, Musiala had already flirted with the German youth set-up, turning out for the national team's under-16s before reverting back to England where he continued to turn out up to under-21 level. When it came to making a definitive choice, the Stuttgart-born winger opted for the country of his birth and has become a beacon of light in a full German team that has been struggling to summon the glories of the Joachim Löw era.

The first leg, at Bayern's Allianz Arena, was another see-saw production, this time Madrid absorbing early home pressure to spring an exquisite sucker-punch goal that saw Toni Kroos play in Vinicius for the finish. A brilliant equaliser from Leroy Sané was followed by a Bayern penalty, won by Musiala and converted by a cool Kane. This despite Bellingham's interference which prompted referee Clément Turpin to intervene and the crowd to react with hostility to the Madrid man. It was a very deliberate piece of gamesmanship, one that could easily have caused friction between two teammates who were set to spend the summer fighting for common cause with their country. Kane brushed the matter off, admitting later: 'In the moment, I didn't know what he said, but I spoke to him after and he said: "I know you're going to go left of the keeper." On the pitch, I knew he was there but I didn't know what he said. But I went left anyway. It was nice for me because I saw the keeper go a little bit early and I put it away.' Had he missed, the repercussions might have been different, but the night ended up finely balanced as Vinicius returned the favour at the other end when Rodrygo was felled by Kim Min-jae.

Madrid had been crowned La Liga champions before the second leg, the perfect tonic ahead of a battle royal at the Bernabéu. Just as Lunin had been required to keep Madrid steady in the first game, so Manuel Neuer came to the fore with a string of saves that frustrated Los Blancos. When Alphonso Davies whacked the ball past Lunin it looked as if Thomas Tuchel might have successfully rumbled Ancelotti, but the coaches' respective use of the substitutes' bench decided the tie. After a conflab with son Davide, Ancelotti signalled for Brahim Díaz and Joselu to come forward with

Rodrygo and Valverde making way. In response, and with only five minutes remaining, Tuchel decided he needed to defend the lead and withdrew Kane and Musiala for the more industrious Thomas Müller and Eric Choupo-Moting. Three minutes later and Joselu was knocking home the rebound after Neuer fumbled the save from a tame Vinicius shot to apparently take the game into extra time . . .

Instead Madrid surfed the wave of euphoria sweeping the stadium to push for a second. Toni Rüdiger crossed from the left, Joselu finished and had barely begun celebrating when the referee ratified the assistant's flag for offside. A VAR review overturned that decision and the Madrid bench erupted, flooding the pitch in delirium. They'd clearly been confident for after the match the players changed into specially commissioned T-shirts emblazoned with the phrase 'a pro la 15'. For the 15th. A club that from top to toe believes in its destiny.

The show moved to London, where the 2024 edition of Europe's premier club fixture had plenty of individual sub-plots with Jude Bellingham and Toni Kroos at the top of the billing. Borussia Dortmund versus Real Madrid would have been no one's idea of the ultimate match-up at the start of the season, even less so after the second round of group games in which Dortmund sat bottom of their four-team section with just a point. This untidy form continued through the Bundesliga season, begetting a fifth-place finish, but in Europe, coach Edin Terzić had managed to tap into something special.

Heading to Wembley as a special guest of Dortmund, Paul Lambert's allegiances were clear and he even made a pre-arranged appearance on TNT's pre-match show regaled in black and yellow. Yet in a certain way he was also rooting for the young man whom Dortmund had sold to Madrid less than a year earlier. And he fully expected him to rise to the occasion. 'Jude plays as though he is still having unbelievable fun,' he said. 'He does the same things now as he did at Birmingham; it's engrained. He thrives on the pressure. Loves the adulation. I was the same. When you hit that level you love the pressure. People used to ask me what it was like to go into a Champions League final with that on your shoulders. It was brilliant! Listen, people *can* capitulate under that. But I loved it because I never ever felt intimidated at any ground, in any game. Even in tunnels before games, if I saw Zidane or Rivaldo, Ballack, Effenberg, Thomas Häßler or whoever, it never bothered me. And I knew what I had round about me. When you have great players on your side, your game becomes better. Jude spent his first season at Madrid with Modrić and Toni Kroos. For me Toni Kroos could play with his suit on. I've never seen him break sweat. He had such a great knack of never giving the ball away.'

On 21 May 2024, Kroos had announced his retirement from football, following through on an earlier promise that Real Madrid would be his last club. As such, the Champions League final would be his swansong with Los Blancos although an earlier decision to step out of international retirement would stand, allowing him to finish his career on home soil with the German national team at Euro 2024. Forty-eight hours before the match, Madrid touched down at Luton Airport, not the most glamorous entrance for the aristocrats in their designer suits, but convenient nonetheless. Bellingham's previous public appearance in the town had come as he helped Birmingham see out a 2-1 victory at Kenilworth Road in January 2020 as a second-half substitute.

Bellingham has become used to being serenaded by Paul McCartney's 1968 singalong composition 'Hey Jude', and footage emerged in the build-up of Madrid and Dortmund fans joining in a chorus of the song on the London Underground. Yet The Beatles do not have a monopoly on Merseyside anthems. Twenty minutes before kick-off, the Dortmund fans were encouraged to sing along to an anthem popularised by Gerry and the Pacemakers and most commonly associated with Liverpool FC. Appropriately, former Dortmund boss Jürgen Klopp, fresh from his departure from Anfield, was among those swaying along to a rendition that stirred and served as a reminder to the Madrid players still warming up that in the stands at least, their club would not be dominating this occasion. The sight and sound of the Yellow Wall, reassembled brick by brick in North London, belting out the song felt organic sitting next to the evening's next pre-match act.

Football's ever-advancing move towards commercialism has thus far eschewed the worst elements of razzamatazz associated with sport in North America, that most capitalist of continents. Yet the introduction of a preening Lenny Kravitz to a stage surrounded by dancers was too much for the BVB fans who felt, with some justification, that they were quite capable of creating their own big-game atmosphere without the enforced revelry of a Super Bowl-style build-up. Those charged with laying on the 'entertainment' pressed on regardless, turning the equivalent of a fire hose on the chanting supporters by blasting the irritating 'Freed

From Desire' (mildly entertaining at Euro 2016) just as the fans at both ends were finding top voice before kick-off. Much more appealing was the moment when Riedle and Zidane brought out the trophy to signal the beginning of proceedings proper.

Bellingham quickly found himself the subject of a flurry of unwanted attention, initially from the cringeworthy advances of a pitch invader stopping for a selfie and more painfully when Dortmund midfielders Emre Can and Marcel Sabitzer took it in turns to foul him. Not that the Germans were exclusively on a mission to spoil. Terzić's game plan saw Dortmund cut open the favourites with Karim Adeyemi's pace exasperating Dani Carvajal while Niclas Füllkrug hit the post with the best effort of the first half. Stationed at the top of a midfield diamond with Kroos at its base and Valverde and Camavinga on either side, Bellingham's familiar role was to link with Rodrygo and Vinicius – and exploit any space he might find around the South American duo. Yet he was finding it hard.

Perhaps this was the night when the lack of a dedicated central striker would finally bite Ancelotti. Where Füllkrug was occupying Nacho and Rüdiger, and giving his side a strong and determined focal point, Bellingham's propensity to wander looking for scraps was not having any marked impact. One wonders what Füllkrug might have made of the cross, slung over by Vinicius, that saw Bellingham leap ahead of keeper Gregor Kobel yet fail to connect when even a glance would surely have claimed the breakthrough goal.

And then the big moment. Kroos dispatched a pinpoint corner to the near post area where Carvajal made a firm and perfectly arrowed connection to head his team into the lead. Madrid had done it again, fashioning a lead when the flow and cadence of the game had suggested an entirely different outcome. What followed suited Ancelotti's serial winners to a tee. Suddenly desperate, Dortmund's play became just that little less measured, their passing imprecise. Madrid seized on those lapses and were suddenly pelting Kobel's goal. And when the normally diligent left-back Ian Maatsen played a loose square pass directly to Bellingham, the game was up. One more basic touch was needed to shuffle the ball to Vinicius and, even as the Brazilian received the ball, Bellingham's hands were aloft in anticipation of the finish which duly found the back of the net. Job done, Bellingham was substituted for Joselu and departed blowing kisses to the Madridistas, before Kroos made a more emotionally stirring departure departing the club stage for the final time to give Modrić the opportunity to take part.

As the final whistle sounded, Bellingham, perhaps for the first time in his career, looked utterly overwhelmed. As the celebrations escalated he turned one way then another, eventually acknowledging the call of Ancelotti and bowing deferentially to the man who'd guided him so adroitly through his first year. There was also a moment with Terzić, who showed grace to take a few moments to congratulate Bellingham on his success. The Dortmund coach later expanded on that conversation, saying: 'When he left us I said the same thing that I said to Erling Haaland – that I was proud to be their manager. I was there when they won the first title of their careers, the German Cup in 2021, and I was quite sure that I won't be around when they win the Champions League. Erling did it last season and unfortunately I was here when Jude won it. It's a very proud moment for him so congratulations to the whole family. I know what Mark, Denise and Jobe are doing to get this success in the family.'

Jude initially struggled to locate his usual poise in front of the camera. His voice shaking with emotion he began: 'I've always dreamed of playing in these games. You go through life and there's so many people who say you can't do things. It gets a bit hard at times and you wonder is it worth it. Nights like tonight make you realise . . . I was all right until I saw my mum and dad's face(s) there . . . nights where they could have been at home by seven and they are doing trips at 11, 12 at night to take me to football. And my little brother who I'm trying to be a role model for. I can't put into words. It's the best night of my life. We missed out on the Copa del Rey, that's the only thing. I'm so grateful. This is a massive group effort and I just can't believe it.'

Denise, Mark and Jobe had first occupied their seats a full five hours before kick-off and made their way afield as the celebrations developed. It's Denise who's been most closely involved in Jude's journey, and as the pair met soon she was sporting his winner's medal – and clutching his match shirt from the biggest night in his career. It was an almost throwaway line, but one was tempted to consider exactly who the doubters were that said Jude 'can't do things'. Was something eating him?

The following day the Madrid squad were back at the Plaza de Cibeles for their latest round of celebrations at the fountain. Madrid had only ever won the league and European double three times before. They had never completed a Champions League campaign unbeaten. Moreover they had only lost twice all season, both in the febrile circumstances of the local derby with Atlético. An uncommon treble of La Liga, Super Cup and Champions League had been secured and Florentino Pérez was delighted to pay tribute to his manager. 'Thank you, Don Carlo, you are the best manager in the world,' he smiled before adding a sting in the tail to the presidential address: '. . . we have now started working to win number 16.'

Chapter 9

ENGLAND EXPECTS

ON THE eve of the Euro 2024 kick-off, tournament sponsors Adidas launched a new promotional advert. Laced
with emotion and soundtracked by an isolated live vocal
from Paul McCartney, the sportswear firm tugged on the
heartstrings as they pushed forward the young starlet they
backed to end nearly 60 years of English hurt.

The clip starts with a family huddled round a television
set as Brian Moore's economical, anguished commentary
describes Paul Gascoigne's semi-final miss against Germany
at Euro '96. As a series of glum faces appear on screen,
McCartney's 'Hey Jude' arrives and we're fast-forwarded in
time to a wistful Frank Lampard sitting in a car reliving
the moment when the officials failed to award a goal in the
2010 World Cup when his long-range shot came crashing down off the bar and over the line. And then there's
a pensive David Beckham, sitting in a darkened room as
rain lashes off a window, his misdemeanours at France '98
hanging gloomily in the air. The mood lifts at the point
when footage of an impish child dribbling and scoring for
Birmingham City's academy team gives way to the clack of
studs in an empty tunnel and a familiar silhouette. The dam

breaks as a commentator hails a Jude Bellingham goal and the song's 'na-na-na-nah' refrain kicks in and is chanted by a full stadium. Eventually the screen cuts to darkness, with Bellingham's face illuminated next to a three-word message emblazoned in capitals: 'YOU GOT THIS'. No pressure.

*

Having made his mark up to under-17 level, the question was when, not if, Jude would be fast-tracked towards full England honours. The under-21 squad is traditionally the finishing school for international hopefuls and, based in the Birmingham area, Aidy Boothroyd was perfectly placed to keep his eye on Jude during his breakout season in the City first team. 'He was Birmingham's star player but it's always difficult to know,' says Boothroyd. 'I was out watching him play but I'd take in a mixture of matches. I might be at a Premier League game one day, a Championship fixture the next, maybe even a German game. The question was how do you gauge a player who is playing 20 or 30 games in the Championship against one who is only just making the bench at Premier League level? It's not an exact science but you use your experience, and we'd get round the table at St George's and talk it through. Jude could play central midfield, wide midfield, off the front, up front or as a centre-back. He is just one of those Rolls-Royce players that come along every now and again. He could play anywhere. He really was that good. We knew he needed to be fast-tracked, it was just a question of timing.'

The call-up for the 21s effectively saw Jude leapfrog four levels, but with the fixture calendar and Covid conspiring to keep the team out of action for ten months, it did not actually materialise until he'd completed his transfer to Borussia. In August 2020, as he settled into a new life, he was summoned to attend for the European Championship qualifiers against Kosovo and Austria. 'My first personal interactions actually came when I met Jude's mum and dad,' continues Boothroyd. 'Obviously any parent is a big influence on their son's career, but the way they went about their business was very professional. You didn't see agents knocking about. They respected the boundaries of England and were so easy to deal with. When he got in the 21s there was a lot of press attention around him, but if his mum and dad didn't want him to do something through the media then he didn't. Everything was carefully planned.'

The Bellinghams may have been able to affect the FA's media policy, but their influence stopped when it came to team selection. 'There's a steeliness about Jude,' continues Boothroyd. 'He doesn't go round telling everybody how good he is – that's obvious to see, you just have to watch him play. For that game against Kosovo I was mixing it up a little, looking at players in different positions. Before reading the team out I pulled Jude to the side and told him he was going to play a bigger part in the second game. There was a look in his eye that said: "Oh, so you're not starting me then!" He didn't say it but there was that look and I thought: "Oh, I like you!" Behind those eyes there is an inner belief. He was like: "That's okay, I'll do that."'

Staged in Pristina, the game was not particularly troubling for Boothroyd's team. By the time Jude appeared they led by three, thanks to a hat-trick from Eddie Nketiah of Arsenal. The substitute wasn't to be upstaged. Already the youngest player to represent England at this level, he also made it on to the scoresheet with a thumping finish to round off a 6-0 victory. 'He was sensational,' admits Boothroyd. 'He had a little cameo of about 25 minutes, scored a goal and made another, and I thought, "Wow." You're playing Kosovo so you've got to take it in context, but the way this kid went about his business, we all knew when we saw him in that game that he needed to be stretched and pushed on to a higher level.'

As promised, a start followed in the game against Austria a few days later, a 2-1 success that nudged the team closer to qualification. A month later the group reconvened, but there was an unexpected blip in the shape of a 3-3 draw in Andorra, a game in which Bellingham appeared from the bench. Restored to the starting line-up for the home game against Turkey he helped the team to a 2-1 win that secured qualification. Already Southgate was hovering.

Boothroyd named Bellingham in the next camp, but there was a surprise in store when the young midfielder checked in at St George's Park. 'I came home the day before and got to see my family which was brilliant,' recalled Jude. 'I was then in the 21s bubble and had just had my Covid swab when Aidy comes up and says: "Gareth wants you for this camp." I was like: "What do you mean? For training?" All of a sudden I just got so nervous. Out of nowhere, two or three hours later I was training with the England senior team.'

Boothroyd would later complain that being England's under-21 boss was akin to an impossible task as he faced up to a tournament minus the services of not only Bellingham but also Phil Foden, Mason Mount and Reece James, each promoted to the senior squad. The 2021 finals were his third in the job, but he quit after a defeat to Croatia sealed the team's elimination at the group stage. 'If Gareth wanted a player he got him,' he says. 'And that was my job as the under-21 coach, not only to give players international experiences but to push, develop and stretch them. We were very proud of our record at the 21s. Not just in terms of the team and qualification but the number of players we got through. The system is working when Trent Alexander-Arnold, Reece James, Jordan Pickford all get a taste and then you have your talents like Foden and Jude who are the best two players I have ever worked with. Jude's reaction to being called up is him right there in a nutshell. That's a lovely way to be. All Jude needed was an opportunity to show everyone what he is all about. He is going to have some bumps and bruises along the way, but he has a great team behind him. When he tells you that he wants to be the best player in the world, that is what he wants to do. He's real, mate. There's no BS with him. He is just a genuine, humble young man, but if he has something to say he will say it.'

Not only was Jude being invited to train with the senior squad, but he was being primed for a first full international cap. In a parallel world he might have been on the other side at Wembley as the Republic of Ireland visited for a friendly. In another universe there might even have been a crowd there to witness what was about as low-key an England debut as you'll ever witness. England were already three goals up, including one from his Dortmund teammate Jadon Sancho, when he was summoned from the sidelines to replace Mount.

Later, Jude would reflect on the night as 'probably

the biggest moment of my life. The number of people who dream of England, the number of players who play Premier League and Champions League and still never get to do it. It was just surreal. It happened so quickly. One minute I was sitting in the stand and then it's "Get ready, you're going on." I've always felt comfortable coming off the bench. And not having fans in the stadium was almost helpful. I was calmer and clearer in my thoughts which made it a bit easier.' This brief introduction made him, at 17 years and 136 days, the third youngest England player of all time after Theo Walcott and Wayne Rooney. 'Wayne Rooney and Steven Gerrard were my heroes,' he added. 'My first England kit had Rooney on the back.'

Although it had been injuries to Trent Alexander-Arnold and James Ward-Prowse that opened the door, Southgate was happy with what he'd seen. Bellingham would not be dropping back down to add to his under-21 cap tally of four. Four months later he made his competitive debut in a World Cup qualifier against San Marino, and in June 2021 he made his first start in a warm-up match for the delayed Euro 2020 finals, playing the 90 minutes in a win over Austria. As the youngest member of Southgate's squad for the tournament he might have been expected to fill a watch and learn brief, yet in the very first game, with England protecting a 1-0 lead against a Croatian team that had knocked England out of the previous World Cup at the semi-final stage, he was sent on to help close the game out. Further substitute appearances against the Czech Republic and Ukraine would follow as England built momentum to reach the final, where they would ultimately lose to Italy on penalty kicks.

Jonathan Northcroft, chief football correspondent at the *Sunday Times* since 2009, is a veteran of the England beat and has written books on the national team. With perhaps the notable exception of Rooney, he has scarcely encountered a player as impactful as Bellingham. 'When Jude came in ahead of the Euros it seemed bold because he was still very young,' he says. 'It wasn't a surprise in the context of Gareth Southgate as he always tried to pick players ahead of their time. That's how he saw the job. But he was 17 and it still felt bold. You were aware another manager wouldn't have done this. And he had more of an impact, more minutes, in the tournament than you would have imagined. It was clearly based on excellence. Both in what he was doing in training and what he was doing when he was on the pitch. It wasn't like he came into a failing team. That's at a successful tournament and he was jostling his way in. That told you the hype is correct that this guy clearly has something special about him. You draw a contrast with someone like Theo Walcott being part of the 2006 squad at 17 and then not playing a minute because they got to Germany and realised that actually the kid was not ready. It was the opposite with Jude. He was ready and you could see that.'

Bellingham did not see any game time during the final itself, but Southgate was envisaging a greater role for the young midfielder as priorities shifted back to qualification for the next major tournament in Qatar. With the world still catching up after the pandemic and the 2022 World Cup occurring in mid-season to counter the effects of the Middle Eastern sun, the football calendar was in a state of congestion. Southgate's team made light work of qualifying with Bellingham picking up additional caps against Andorra, Albania and San Marino, but once qualified, there was another competition to fit in. Designed to reduce the number of meaningless friendlies, the UEFA Nations League has been useful to smaller countries eager to accelerate their qualification prospects.

For England, it's been harder to divine the benefits and for Southgate, this latest edition was to become a fraught business. Draws against Germany and Italy were no disgrace, but would have been far easier to stomach had they not been bookended by defeats to Hungary, the second of which was a 4-0 defeat at Wembley. Still waiting to celebrate his 19th birthday, Bellingham started both those matches but was spared the worst of the scrutiny, which only grew when relegation from League A was confirmed after a defeat to Italy in Milan later in the year. An unused substitute in the San Siro, Bellingham was nevertheless moving up a gear for Borussia Dortmund. Season three was his strongest in Germany and his game moved to a dynamic new level under the guidance of Edin Terzić.

Southgate was happy to embrace this upsurge and handed the 19-year-old a starting berth for the World Cup. He rewarded that faith by registering England's first of the tournament in the 6-2 win over Iran in Al Rayyan. Wearing his beloved No. 22 jersey, the midfielder's first senior international goal arrived via a well-directed header from Luke Shaw's cross.

'The process between the two tournaments was pretty rocky,' continues Northcroft. 'There was a great initial qualifying performance then the disastrous Nations League in the summer. So England arrived into the World Cup with a few question marks. But they were brilliant from the start and Jude was on it and important. He played as the third midfielder, the most attacking one, striding forward from midfield almost Gascoigne-style. He gave the team a new dimension and I think that tournament is the best the team ever played under Gareth Southgate.'

Chris Powell, who served as an assistant coach under Southgate at both Euro 2020 and the World Cup, was startled by Bellingham's impact. He said: 'Scoring the first goal in that World Cup got us going as there was a lot of pressure on that game and we were expected to win. Every game he got better and better. In camp, during the Euros all you ever heard was "well played, Jude", "fantastic, Jude", "well played, Bellers". It came from everyone, the players, coaches, staff. I think he put a marker down. That he was here to stay for a long time. It was just uncanny watching a player who had a real idea of the game. I think he knocked on Gareth's door which rarely anyone does! And they had their conversation about training and about him being more involved. Gareth knew his time would come and got him used to how to be an England player. He is demanding of everyone, (even) more established players, senior pros, He'd say: "I want it to be better, Chris."'

Free-flowing in that opening fixture, England were held to a goalless deadlock by the USA in game two, but rediscovered some fluency in the third match to beat Wales 3-0. Marcus Rashford (2) and Phil Foden may have claimed the goals, but Bellingham was asserting his authority. 'The relationships he had with other players, particularly Jordan Henderson, were important and striking,' adds Northcroft. 'By the end of that tournament you thought he was more or less the most important player in the team. He was a leader if not the leader. And it was never more striking than in the game against France.'

Before facing the reigning champions, England first faced Senegal in the round of 16, with Bellingham to the fore with an assist for Henderson's opener, a goal which prompted the two to indulge in a ritualistic head-butting celebration, and then another key contribution for the second, his driving run from deep eliminating four players and freeing Foden to assist for Harry Kane's simple finish. The eventual 3-0 win was comprehensive, but something special would be needed to see off the French in the quarter-finals. Southgate's team couldn't quite muster enough, but Bellingham was ceaseless in his efforts to try and figure a way through. His future Real Madrid teammate Aurélien Tchouaméni gave France the lead and Olivier Giroud claimed the winner with two Kane penalties – one scored and one missed – completing the tale of the tape. England didn't quite have enough but Bellingham had confirmed himself as a player for the big stage.

'When England were under the most pressure against the best team they faced, and when they were in difficulty, he was leading and demanding of other players,' recalls Northcroft. 'I watched the game back and it was striking what he was doing; the youngest player on the team was trying to boss people. And trying to resist defeat the most. That's when you really saw his personality properly come out, his high standards and his drive. After Jordan Henderson he was the most vocal and demanding player on the pitch and that really struck you given his age. I came out of that tournament thinking Jude Bellingham is going to be the main figure of this team going forward. Most players by the time they are playing internationals will have been really tested at club level in terms of cup finals or title deciders. Jude had limited exposure to those types of games. Those World Cup games would have been the biggest games he'd played in his life. Maybe there is a parallel with Wayne Rooney, whose games at Euro 2004 were far bigger than anything he'd had with Everton and he stepped up pretty effortlessly. And by the way I don't want to overhype Jude. Jude's impact in 2022 wasn't anything like Rooney's impact in 2004, so I do think we need a bit of perspective. For all that he is an extraordinary talent, I don't think his trajectory in purely international terms is the same as Wayne Rooney's. In club terms it is a totally different story.'

Rooney would go on to break Bobby Charlton's all-time goalscoring record for England, but in club terms he operated as a home bird, transferring the short distance from Merseyside to Manchester United where he spent the bulk of his career. There were chances to move abroad – Real Madrid and Barcelona were both keen to rival Chelsea for his signature during a contract impasse – but he did not leap until the twilight of his career, spending a year in the States with DC United. By contrast there's nothing to suggest that Bellingham harbours any great desire to play in England's top flight. After helping his country defeat Italy in a Euro 2024 qualifier, he stated that he would love to spend the next 'ten to fifteen years' in Madrid.

Yet his club priorities need not be confused with a lack of patriotism. The first international window following his move to Spain included a trip to Glasgow for a re-enactment of the first ever international fixture against Scotland. It was England who looked sharper and hungrier. And as the game developed, one player emerged as the boss, having a big hand in each of his team's three goals. After capitalising on a mistake from Andy Robertson to score the second, Bellingham defiantly landed in his celebratory stance.

'If I'm thinking of Jude Bellingham's iconic moments so far, that game would be really high on the scale,' says Northcroft. 'He embraced that game better than anyone on the England team. The first 20 minutes were actually quite difficult for him. He was getting a lot of physical attention, trying things that weren't necessarily coming off and the crowd were getting on at him. And his response was to go up a gear. To score, to celebrate the way he did and then to boss the game really. And relish it and love it. For me the weight of that celebration really hit home for the first time because it was someone playing in the lions' den and scoring and then in front of the very crowd that is heckling him saying: "Come on then, I'm the guy." It was brave. I don't know if an England player has ever celebrated like that at Hampden before.'

Injury would restrict his involvement in the remaining Euro 2024 qualifiers, but he was back in the squad for spring friendlies against Brazil and Belgium. Overshadowed by future Madrid teammate Endrick, who added a Wembley winner to his list of achievements at just 17, Bellingham felt the need to speak out in defence of Southgate after his third international goal spared the team another home defeat against the Belgians. 'I liked it because I know the rubbish we would have got if we'd lost two games on the bounce,' he said of his goal. 'I know people will be negative but you have to take these games for what they are. You've got to keep perspective. Of course it's hard for the gaffer. People need to realise how hard it is.'

For Boothroyd, who'd broken the good news of his full international promotion just three years previously, this intervention was something to behold. 'He said some very mature things that night,' says Boothroyd. 'He's only had a few caps and he's almost protecting the England manager! I thought: "Brilliant, kid, well done."'

Chapter 10

WHO ELSE?

ADIDAS will have paid well for the privilege of utilising Jude in their promotional film, but they weren't exactly discouraging the lad to carry the world upon his shoulders. And doubtless someone at the sports manufacturer's HQ in Bavaria took great delight in highlighting just how often England's tournament failure seemed to be intertwined with the success of their German rivals. Little matter, it was only an ad. And hadn't Gareth Southgate once appeared in a pizza advert, sending himself up for his own missed penalty against the Germans in that Euro '96 semi?

If you were to listen to some of the insinuation and innuendo circulating around the England camp come the end of Euro 2024, you might be forgiven for reckoning that the promo film was an unforgivable act of self-indulgence that upset team harmony. Such are the perils of being involved with a national team that has won nothing since hosting the World Cup in 1966, yet has never got used to the sensation of losing. Every second summer a similar theme emerges. Of how this might be the time for England to finally lay the ghost of '66 to rest and set a new benchmark.

Invariably, the hype has borne little relation to the actual quality of the players in any given year, save perhaps for 2004 when the so-called Golden Generation set off for Portugal. Managed by the light touch of the avuncular Sven-Göran Eriksson and boasting a squad packed to the gunnels with ability, England swaggered into the tournament with arguably the finest array of talent it had ever had at its disposal. Yet for Messrs Beckham, Lampard and Gerrard there never was to be that moment of international glory. In 18-year-old Wayne Rooney, Eriksson's team had a boy wonder of its own and Rooney played like the best striker in the world in the group stage, rattling in four goals before England were ousted by the hosts after a penalty shoot-out in the quarter-finals. The sight of a functional but limited Greece team eventually picking up the trophy deepened the sense of regret.

Pre-tournament favourites for the 2024 jamboree in Germany, similar predictions were being made of Southgate's young team. Edged out from the 12-yard mark as the Covid-delayed edition of the tournament crescendoed in a final at Wembley three years earlier, England arrived into the summer looking even stronger than they did when pitted against Italy with home advantage in 2021. Captain and chief goalscorer Harry Kane was operating at the peak of his powers with Bayern Munich. Phil Foden had turned in a sublime season for champions Manchester City to be named the Premier League's player of the year. Bukayo Saka and Declan Rice moved to another level of performance as part of an ever-improving Arsenal team that pushed City all the way. And then there was Bellingham, just 17 and a mere squad member when the last Euros kicked off, now coming into the summer as a Champions League winner with Real Madrid. The ingredients were there for England to have a proper crack at the competition and, having gone so close last time out, why shouldn't this enhanced team fancy its chances? History advised caution.

Back in 2004, Eriksson could select a midfield of Beckham, Gerrard, Lampard and Paul Scholes behind a front two of 2001 Ballon d'Or winner Michael Owen and the country's new wonderkid. Yet for all Rooney's effervescence, the blend behind him was never quite right. Captain Beckham was a model of efficiency on the right, but Eriksson could never perfect the mix between the other three.

Southgate was similarly well stocked from middle to front, but while Eriksson could call upon elite level defenders like Rio Ferdinand, Sol Campbell and Ashley Cole, on current form only Kyle Walker could be placed in the same bracket. All the more reason surely for Southgate to maximise the abundance of riches available at the other end of the pitch. Few teams in the tournament would swap out their centre-forward for Kane, while Bellingham and Foden are arguably the two best attacking midfielders in the world. As he pondered how to succeed where Eriksson failed, would Southgate come to believe that being bold was also the practical option?

With the experienced Harry Maguire and Jordan Henderson missing for this tournament, Southgate constructed a new four-man leadership group around captain Harry Kane, with vice-captain Kyle Walker, Rice and Bellingham joining the committee. Jude would not celebrate his 21st birthday until four days after England played their final group match against Slovenia, but he was now officially a senior player.

There was some misdirection in the very structure of Southgate's provisional squad announcement in which Bellingham was listed as a 'forward'. Wearing No. 10 and nominally deployed in the position to match, Bellingham instead played as a roving 22 in England's tournament opener against Serbia. One moment he was dropping deep to demand the ball from the toes of his centre-backs, the next breaking beyond Kane to find some space in the final third. The game had barely settled into a rhythm when he both started and ended the move that gave England the lead against a grisly Serbian side that had already been taking turns to clatter the chief. The forcefulness of the run and leap as he crashed through Andrija Živković to meet Bukayo Saka's cross was a true statement of intent. The rest of the half was a tour de force as Bellingham ran, tackled – and sledged – like he was on a one-man mission to dismantle the opposition. A subdued Kane might have been pondering whether to hand over the armband on the spot. There were some stunning moments of skill too, not least in one volleyed cross-field pass he slung out to Kieran Trippier with the outside of his foot.

It was another landmark night for Jude, one on which he became the first European player under 21 to have played in three major international tournaments. The adjudication process for the player of the match award could not have taken long, yet there was a tapering off in his energy and performance in the second half. Not a problem in itself, but the next few matches offered wearying signs that this tournament might have been an assignment too far. 'The first half-hour was sensational,' observes Northcroft. 'He played like the king of the team, the best player in the playground who takes the ball off everyone and does whatever he wants across the pitch. But of course he couldn't sustain it. It was like watching a boxer who has punched himself out and he was then visibly clinging on for the rest of the game. You could say that the first half an hour showed how great he is or that the game showed how young he is because he didn't know how to pace himself properly. But he will learn.'

Match day two against Denmark was always likely to be a tougher, stuffier affair. Southgate's team laboured their way to a 1-1 draw in Frankfurt that, in truth, was boring. Once again, Bellingham was treated to some forceful tackling, but managed to keep his frustration in check partly, one was tempted to conclude, because of UEFA's tournament directive of only allowing team captains to approach the referee. Overall, it was a leggy performance from England and the post-match debate centred largely on the two issues of goalscorer Kane's effectiveness and the midfield mix.

With qualification for the knockout phase already secure, Southgate made only a minor tweak for the final group match against Slovenia, introducing Conor Gallagher in place of Trent Alexander-Arnold in the middle of the park. Yet it was not until the half-time introduction of teenager Kobbie Mainoo, and the later additions of Cole Palmer and Anthony Gordon, that England really started to carry a persistent threat. Even when the tempo lifted, Jude struggled to get going and by the night's end his statistics were not impressive. Not only had he failed to register a shot, or create a chance for a teammate, he had also prevailed in only 22 per cent of his individual duels. This was not the Bellingham everyone had come to know and admire.

The group stage of Euro 2024 had been a competition of extremes, with players at either end of the age spectrum excelling. The Madrid connection was writ large. A vibrant Portugal side was not only captained by the 39-year-old Cristiano Ronaldo, but marshalled at the back by another former Madridista, the 41-year-old Pepe who seemed to be snuffing out fires via mind control. Hosts Germany had brought Toni Kroos out of international retirement for one final goodbye after his announcement that he would not be seeking a new club following his departure from Madrid. Yet coach Julian Nagelsmann was also looking to the future with Jamal Musiala and Florian Wirtz a whirl of thrilling movement and invention. Behind them, pass-master Kroos was in his element. Turkey were helped to the quarter-finals by 18-year-old Arda Güler, who scored one of the goals of the tournament in perhaps the game of the tournament, a nail-biting group match against Georgia in Dortmund.

Perhaps best of all was Barcelona's 16-year-old Lamine Yamal, who was doing his homework between training sessions in the Spanish training camp at Donaueschingen then lighting up matches with his impudent wing play. By comparison, Bellingham seemed to be running on fumes. Speaking to the *Lions' Den*, an in-house show broadcast on the FA's YouTube channel, Bellingham confessed to having felt 'absolutely dead' during the final group game against Slovenia. It was a frank admission and not one to inspire reassurance as the tournament entered the serious business of the knockout phase.

On Saturday 29 June, the eve of the round of 16 encounter with Slovakia in Gelsenkirchen, Jude celebrated his 21st birthday. He did so not to a backdrop of celebration but concern, certainly in the eyes of the opinion formers of the English media. Southgate had spoken of blocking out the noise within camp, while Bellingham had remarked on that YouTube appearance that the only views that affected him and his teammates were those of the fans inside the stadiums whom he regarded as being universally supportive. He must have missed the plastic cups rained in Southgate's direction at the conclusion of the Slovenia match. And the column penned by Wayne Rooney in *The Times* was not so much a Happy Birthday message as a warning. Opening with a critique on Jude's body language that 'left me worried', Rooney went on to implore the young midfielder to stop trying too hard. He continued: 'I know it's hard. He reminds me of myself in tournaments where you want so desperately to do well and know you and the team could be playing better, and it gets to you. But don't do something stupid, Jude.' Rooney was making reference to the red card he received in the 2006 quarter-final against Portugal, a moment that effectively ended England's hopes of prevailing on their last big competition visit to German soil.

Although Rooney delivers his words under the old-media masthead of *The Times*, the majority of those who consumed his words would have done so online, either through a subscription or the subsequent mass cutting and pasting of his words to every conceivable football website hungry for clicks. Still young enough to have played in the era of Twitter and Facebook, Rooney's roots were nevertheless in a more analogue world when the views of the

British news-stand still held sway. The red-top hysteria that held enough sway to damage the career prospects of Bobby Robson and Graham Taylor in the 1990s may have subsided, but as recently as 2016, a *Daily Telegraph* sting had been powerful enough to take down Southgate's immediate predecessor, Sam Allardyce. While the old adage of 'never make war with a man who buys his ink by the barrel' may have lost some relevance, the influence of the English newsmen was still significant.

Ever thoughtful and holistic in his approach to management, Southgate had acknowledged that fact by dedicating time and effort into building bridges with journalists across his reign, in the process removing cynicism on the other side and reducing suspicion and fear within. The relationship had been detoxified over time through initiatives such as American-style media open days and darts competitions between players and reporters. Yet for all the universal admiration of Jude's public persona, his media appearances, dating back to his Birmingham days, had always been carefully curated, his exposure to journalists limited and timed to specific occasions such as post-match interviews with television rights holders.

In Germany there was a growing feeling among those assigned to cover the tournament that, while perfectly capable of holding his own in public, Jude was being afforded a get-out as certain teammates took up the slack. Word around the camp suggested that parental guidance was still at play, with Team Bellingham being granted a veto around Jude's interview commitments, this itself seemingly at odds with the more open and less cynical culture fostered by Southgate throughout his reign.

'I find it strange that, up to now, he has hardly done any media interviews and I would hope that situation changes,' continued Rooney. 'He is in England's leadership group and, whether he likes it or not, he is a talisman for his country now; he has just won La Liga and the Champions League and is in a position where he should be taking responsibility.' In a sense Bellingham couldn't win. A week after Rooney suggested he should be fronting up with the media, Graeme Souness was using his own Saturday column in the *Daily Mail* to criticise the 21-year-old for having too much to say. In this regard he was probably unique among the England squad; anything he did say was likely to be amplified to a volume far louder than that of any of his teammates, his words shared in far higher numbers and dissected with greater scrutiny.

Paid columnists like Rooney and Souness were not alone in offering a critical view and the 90-plus minutes offered up in the Arena AufSchalke by Southgate's tentative group served only to strengthen the case for the dissent. The spectacular, potentially summer-defining pay-off delivered by Bellingham to save England's tournament only served to illustrate the size of his talent – and his proven knack for delivering on the big occasion.

In a testy, bitty opening to the game, three England players were booked, including Bellingham who was cautioned for a lunge on Slovakia's wide player Lukáš Haraslín. In defiance of the new regulations around player discourse with the match officials, he made his objections known and with little subtlety. This was another turgid performance from England and, worryingly, not even Ivan Schranz's breakthrough goal was enough to raise the energy levels.

As time ticked away, the sense that Bellingham and Phil Foden were not happily coexisting grew stronger. The former grew grumpier as the latter lost heart and neither was producing even a flicker of the creative output with which they'd spoiled their club followers over the previous year. Taken out late by Slovak stopper Milan Škriniar just before half-time, Bellingham left the field having another nibble at the officials' ears while teammates Kieran Trippier, Kobbie Mainoo and Declan Rice all felt the force of his frustration in the second half.

Southgate finally withdrew Foden for Ivan Toney deep into stoppage time and, suddenly, a piece of old-fashioned, unreconstructed desperation forced the equaliser. Kyle Walker's throw was the catalyst and Marc Guehi's flick-on set Bellingham up for his spectacular moment. The volleyed finish was an outrageous explosion of confidence, athleticism and technique as he twisted in mid-air to execute an overhead kick back into the bottom corner. 'Who else?' he mouthed as he ran off towards the touchline to celebrate, eventually being joined by Kane in a dual execution of his celebration stance. Extra time had barely kicked off when Kane was nodding home the winner to put England into the quarter-finals. Bellingham returned the favour by joining in Kane's own signature move.

Even when achingly tired and frustrated, Bellingham had delivered a moment fit to sit alongside the glittering highlights reel assembled during his first season in Madrid. Afterwards, he conducted some flash interviews and also offered some combative words at the post-match press conference. There was a winning sound bite in his 'I do' response to the interviewer who asked him who writes his scripts. But there was also a spicy garnish to his words. He said: 'It's been tough to try and keep the negative energy outside of the camp. Today they will have been ready for us. But we showed the kind of character England has missed. If it ends up being one that helps us lift the cup it will be right up there. I know what I can deliver in those moments, regardless of what people say. I have done it for Madrid this year and I have done it for England. But we won this game together, not me, not Harry.' He added: 'It's a feeling like no other. Because you are 30 seconds from going home, having to listen to all the rubbish, feeling like you have let the nation down. One kick of the ball can change everything. It's a habit I have picked up from Madrid. I'm really grateful I could bring it to this game. Playing for England is enjoyable but there is also a lot of pressure. You hear people talk a lot of rubbish and it's nice that when you deliver you can give them a little bit back. It's very difficult in press conferences and interviews to talk as openly as footballers want to because we are always judged.'

By the time he was next heard in public, this time via the FA's Diary Room forum online, Jude was in humble mode, playing down the technical merit of his wonder goal and eager to spread a little warmth to one of his less-heralded teammates. 'Marc has probably the best flick-on header in England history,' he said of Guehi. 'He will never take any credit for it but it's important he knows how appreciative I am and the team are of his contribution. Marc is just the most humble geezer. I'm really keen on giving people their flowers, especially when they have been as good as he has at this tournament. He has set up a goal that is so important to us as a team. It was really instinct more than anything. It fell in the perfect spot, a little bit behind me. When I was in the air, I thought I'm six feet off the ground and it's like Ronaldo. I watched it back and I've very much still got one arm on the ground! So it wasn't the most acrobatic but I think it was a nice contact, and when I turned round on the floor and saw it rolling in, I thought: "Oh my God!" It was definitely one of the most memorable and important moments of my career so far.'

And yet within 24 hours, Bellingham had been handed a UEFA charge for his conduct during his celebration. Amid the drama and euphoria, he had also made a cupping gesture next to his crotch, antagonising members of the Slovakian bench in the process. Bellingham's later assertion that he was participating in an in-joke with friends cut no ice with the governing body and its Control, Ethics and Disciplinary Body hit him with a €30,000 fine and a one-match ban (suspended for a year) for 'violating the basic rules of decent conduct'. For context, the fine simultaneously issued to the English FA for crowd disturbances was €10,000 with a further €1,000 billed for the lighting of fireworks.

The punishment left Bellingham free to face Switzerland in the quarter-final and he took his place in a rejigged line-up in which Southgate had abandoned his 4-3-3 shape for a 3-4-2-1 which deployed Bellingham and Foden as dual No. 10s. This was Southgate's 100th match in charge of England and it had the potential to be his last, especially when an uninspiring performance started to unravel as Breel Embolo gave Switzerland the lead in Düsseldorf.

High among the loudening complaints about the manager was his unwillingness to make in-game changes quickly enough, and when he reacted with a triple substitution it was a surprise to see the No. 10 being held aloft by the fourth official. Bellingham looked bewildered and seemed to be ignoring the summons even before the officials were instructed to correct their mistake and display the number 14 of Ezri Konsa instead.

Aside from feeling the weight of a few meaty Swiss tackles, it had not been a vintage Bellingham display, but given his moment of genius in the prior fixture, it would have made little sense for Southgate to deny himself the possibility of another, no matter how weary the player. Instead it was Saka who came up with the goods, drilling home a low shot and setting up another 30 minutes of grind through extra time. Still Southgate persisted with Bellingham, quite possibly because he knew he could rely on him to step up and score in a penalty shoot-out. Up second in the order after Cole Palmer, he delivered one of five perfect England penalties to send the team through, hurdling a significant psychological barrier in the process.

Here England were, in a semi-final, without really managing to put together even 45 minutes of play commensurate with the talent available. If one couldn't necessarily regard the team as lucky in any individual match, providence was smiling on Southgate in the mechanics of the tournament with an underwhelming France joining Spain, Portugal and Germany in the other side of the draw. That left England to battle with the Netherlands for a place in the final and for Jude it was also a homecoming of sorts as he returned to Dortmund for the first time since his league heartache a year earlier.

In place of the Yellow Wall stood a cascade of Oranje as noisy Dutch fans assembled and almost immediately seemed to suck Xavi Simons' raking shot into the net behind Pickford. Just seven minutes in and England were in danger of going under and out, yet from somewhere Southgate's team found their best football of the tournament and started to probe and pass their way into a period of dominance. Their enterprise merited an equaliser but the 'infringement' that saw them do so from the penalty spot was patently undeserving.

One heavily dramatised subplot to Jude's Dortmund return surrounded UEFA's decision to appoint Felix Zwayer as referee for the game. Bellingham's outburst against the official caused mere ripples in the English media back in 2022, but suddenly it was back-page news as Zwayer's past indiscretions were laid bare alongside the midfielder's intemperate reaction in the post-match fire of a title race. Just how attuned Zwayer was to this reheated scandal is up for debate, but there seemed little wrong with his instincts when he signalled for a goal kick after Kane had blazed a shot over the bar, before taking a sore one from Denzel Dumfries in the follow-through. The video assistant referee decided the German needed a fresh look at the movement and urged him to visit the pitchside monitor for another look. Regardless of anything dredged up in the build-up, this was suddenly a pressure moment for Zwayer and, after viewing and reviewing the moment several times, he decided that there was indeed something 'clear and obviously' wrong with his initial call and awarded a penalty. No one in camp Bellingham would have been cursing his integrity as Kane drilled home the kick to level the game.

The second half dampened some of the England momentum and Southgate (eventually) reached for his substitutes.

Ollie Watkins, one of those replacements, brought the magic deep in stoppage time with a sharp turn and angled drive that beat Bart Verbruggen to send England through to a second consecutive European final. Bellingham was back at the florists, gathering bouquets to throw at the feet of a teammate. 'I'm so happy for Ollie,' he said. 'I couldn't be prouder of him and as a team we are buzzing for him. Because people don't understand you miss your holidays, you come away without your family and you're not starting every game like you would at your club. It's difficult. It can take a lot out of you if you don't have the right mentality. Ollie has. He's the hero and he's saved us.

'To be back here at this club that helped turn me into the man and the player I am, I'm really grateful. It's special for me. Finding a way, that character, mentality and attitude that anyone can win us the game if they are given the chance. It's something that is built through failure. You are going to get criticised when you don't play well, but it's important that you build that fire and resistance to it and realise we can do better. In games like these we come together like no other team. We've delivered again. These moments bring us together as a team and a family. We live through these moments together and because of that you get stronger. It's about taking that into the final.'

England had once again prevailed on the back of a big moment. And those who had criticised Gareth Southgate for the lack of fluency were overlooking the point that international tournament football often spins on flashes of inspiration and spontaneity. The trouble was that they were about to face the one team in the tournament who were displaying those qualities consistently and in abundance.

*

Before every game, Jude Bellingham follows the same routine. After descending the steps of the team coach he heads for the tunnel and makes a beeline for the centre circle. Once there, he slowly scans his surroundings and absorbs the ambience of the arena he seeks to dominate. Beyond superstition, it's a practice that allows him to visualise the game to come, the match-ups in midfield, the spaces into which he hopes to bound and gain an advantage.

The dimensions of Berlin's Olympic Stadium offer their own peculiar shadows and shapes and there's history steeped into the stone surroundings of a stadium purpose-built for the 1936 Olympics by the Nazis, yet forever remembered for the medal-winning exploits of American sprinter Jesse Owens. After a brief interlude in which his Madrid pal Joselu stopped him for a quick chat and a cuddle, Jude was down on his hunkers, eyes alert and slowly scrolling round the stadium bowl in order to summon those all-important pictures. Perhaps his mind would have floated back to the day he collected his first ever winner's medal on these very premises. A German Cup final conducted in the eerie midst of the Covid pandemic, without a spectator in sight. Yet there were also ghosts stalking the ground.

Berlin last staged a major international final in 2006, when Italy met France in contest for the World Cup. The game is not remembered for the football. Neither is its memory summoned on account of the quality of its goals. The goalscorers are, however, synonymous with one of the game's most incendiary and defining incidents. This was the final match of the great Zinedine Zidane's career and, when the French captain chipped home a delightful Panenka-style dinked penalty kick that clipped the underside of the bar for added dramatic effect, it seemed like the perfect end to a golden story. Marco Materazzi had already done something to ruin Zidane's party by heading home the equaliser, but the Italian defender wasn't done there. Deep into extra time, the pair clashed ostensibly on account of words Materazzi uttered in Zidane's direction. Zidane's response was to assume a bull-like stance and butt his opponent in the chest with his head. It was a spectacularly ugly moment, one at odds with the poise and grace that had characterised Zidane's football. It was also a summary lesson of how even the greatest can be goaded into losing their shape.

Jude Bellingham had idolised Zidane. He'd also been compared to him. And when the time came to rubber-stamp his life-changing move to Real Madrid, he'd happily adopted Zidane's distinctive No. 5 jersey. Here was someone who invited pressure on his shoulders, an uncommon trait among English sportsmen. If he wasn't quite looking to emulate Zidane's moment of infamy, he would have been perfectly comfortable striding on to the stage of Owens or indeed Usain Bolt, who set the 100-metre record time of 9.58 seconds here in the 2009 World Championships.

Yet if England were to prevail, they would need to beat the side which, by common consent, had been the best and most exciting performers in the tournament. Thrown together by Luis de la Fuente during a qualifying campaign that began with defeat to Scotland in Glasgow, Spain had benefited from a complete reinvention around midfield holder Rodri, the unchanged component in a young, vibrant team. Most thrillingly, the introduction of young wingers Lamine Yamal, who'd celebrated his 17th birthday on the eve of the final, and Nico Williams had given Spain the kind of penetration that England fans had craved from their talented yet seemingly inhibited squad. They'd rampaged their way through the tournament and made light of a devilish draw, beating reigning champions Italy, hosts Germany and a strong French team en route to Berlin.

Before kick-off, the trophy was delivered by another man cast from the mould of hard Italian defenders, Giorgio Chiellini, who captained Italy to victory in the previous edition at Wembley three summers previously. Chiellini's presence was another reminder for everyone of the guts and determination and the ability to just *hang in* that is often required to get over the line and close out a successful tournament win.

Southgate made one notable selection decision. Luke Shaw had been England's unlikely scorer in 2021, shocking the Italians with a goal inside two minutes, and that may well have influenced the coach's decision to hand the left-back a first start of the competition – and indeed in any context since he picked up an injury with Manchester United in February. Shaw's inclusion saw the team revert to a back four, and further forward it was Bellingham and not Foden who was asked to move left and assist in defending the dual threat of Yamal and the rampaging Dani Carvajal.

Bellingham was not short on effort. But with Spain dominating the ball his role was to be disciplined in fulfilling his defensive duties rather than probing for the spaces in forward areas. He tackled gamely and took a few hits for his trouble. England just never looked fluent. When they did conjure something, Bellingham was invariably involved, but he was not playing like a man at the peak of his physical powers. England should have got a lift when they realised the injured Rodri, later to be announced as player of the tournament, would not be fit to return for the second half. But, if anything, his replacement Martín Zubimendi proved even more adept at shuffling the ball around and he was there at the root of Spain's opening goal barely a minute after the restart.

England had successfully repressed the threat of Yamal and Nico Williams for the duration of the first half, but the duo combined to devastating effect. Fatally, Shaw took his eye off Yamal for a second and, as the teenager wandered into space inside, Carvajal found him with a quick, first-time pass. Yamal moved off at speed before drilling a pass to his counterpart as he advanced off the opposite flank and into the box. Williams sized up the angle and drilled a finish past Pickford. England were ragged and Spain threatened to run rampant. Jordan Pickford was emerging as England's best player, and for a time Bellingham's best moment had been the show of strength that dispossessed Yamal and the subsequent drop of the shoulder that left the youngster trailing. Trouble was he executed that move inside his own box.

After an hour, Southgate took the big but obvious call to remove his labouring captain Harry Kane and introduce Watkins, yet if England were to get back in it, it seemed likely that Bellingham would be the catalyst. He almost got the leveller at the end of a forceful piece of play in which he utilised brute strength and a magnetic touch to receive and hold off Carvajal on the edge of the box. His left-foot thwack flew only marginally wide.

You could almost have credited Bellingham with two assists at the equaliser. Again he was strong and sure of touch to deal with Pickford's heavy clearance and he took a thump from Marc Cucurella in the process of laying off to Cole Palmer. Just on for Kobbie Mainoo, Palmer sent Bukayo Saka scampering down the right and when the Arsenal man needed a target, there, again, was Bellingham, taking yet another hit as he received and deftly cushioned the ball into Palmer's path to follow up and stroke the finish home from 20 yards. He was now running on fumes yet there was no case for subjecting him to the same fate as Kane. He had to stay on.

There were to be no late heroics this time. A set-piece game of pinball in which Rice and Guehi attempted headers on goal was as close as England came, and Spain were precise and clinical on the counter that settled the game. Sub Mikel Oyarzabal dropped in to pick the ball up centrally, nudged the ball wide into Cucurella's path and spun in behind, meeting the full-back's first-time delivery with a one-touch finish. Bellingham had one last go at forcing something, carrying the ball forward with purpose before finding Watkins with a piercing pass. The striker's touch was not sure enough and the opportunity was lost.

Bellingham wanted no part in the commiserations and trudged for the dugout at full time, leathering a crateful of drinks bottles before slumping into a seat. His head lifted only momentarily to acknowledge Nacho, who'd sought him out and leant into the plastic shelter to offer a warm embrace and some words of consolation. When

Bellingham eventually re-emerged, he was soon back on his hunkers. Then his knees. Various backroom staff briefly approached but exited sharply. As he rejoined the clump of England players ahead of the presentation ceremony, he fell to his back before returning to a crouch and being spotted and papped by a group of busy photographers, eager to capture the definitive misery shot. It was at this point that Southgate approached and delivered a message of his own. Soon Bellingham was doing the round of his teammates before acknowledging the tens of thousands of England fans who'd resisted the temptation to make a sharp exit. And then the Spanish approached, Pedro, Joselu and Rodri all offering empathy ahead of the slow march to the podium for the runners-up baubles. Jude was at the back of the group, marshalled by Southgate, and barely glanced at the trophy as captain Álvaro Morata hoisted it high towards a sky encircled by the ring of red and yellow shone on the horseshoe roof in acclaim of Spain's fourth European crown.

England are still in search of their first. The common opinion of Bellingham's final, if not his tournament, was that England had needed more from him. That he was tired. Both opinions are fair and accurate. But he was also playing in a team that was not set up to maximise his attacking strengths. And so he contributed in other ways. When UEFA's final stats were published, they revealed that Bellingham had, by a considerable margin, made more tackles during the tournament than any other player. He had also been fouled more often than any other player – 16 times across seven games. His goal tally of two was only one short of the modest Golden Boot-winning tally.

In the final analysis, Northcroft also believes that Bellingham's Euro 2024 will not be remembered for the tired football or the crotch-grabbing celebration, but something much closer to the very essence of the game. 'Tournaments are staging posts in people's lives,' he argues. 'When you look back, you remember the tournament you saw as a kid. It's part of how you chart your childhood. There would be a generation of kids watching Euro 2024 who won't remember the rubbish that was said about England and won't remember the toiling performances. They will remember Jude Bellingham's goal. People will ask do you remember where you were when you were watching that overhead kick? That and the Ollie Watkins goal will outlive the tournament. Those are the memories the fans will look back on. You could say, and Gareth Southgate tried to articulate this, that if the national team's job is to bring joy to the people, then this team did provide a couple of moments that are up there with anything. I don't know if England have ever scored a last-minute goal like that. If you were to rerun all the England goals at tournaments and rank them, that would be right up there, if not at the very top.'

At the end of a season in which destiny seemed to call at every turn, he had fallen short. And, as he exited the Olympic Stadium, there was a look of anger in his eyes. It would seem a safe bet that he'll be back.

Chapter 11

A SOCIAL CONSCIENCE

WHEN David Beckham joined the ranks of the Galacticos in 2003, it felt like we were witnessing a new age of super-stardom. Famous as much for his pop star wife, his brand endorsements and his fashion choices as the peerless ball-striking technique of his right boot, Beckham brought a package of benefits that transcended his use to the team of superstars assembled under Florentino Pérez. Seldom had the spotlight shone as intensely on one individual, yet Beckham, pilloried in the English press following his red card for kicking out at Argentina's Diego Simeone in the 1998 World Cup quarter-final in Saint-Etienne, had learned the hard way how to cope with the worst aspects of the media glare.

Effigies of Beckham had been hung in the streets fol-lowing France '98 and, although he showed admirable character to instantly redeem and enhance his reputation in a silver-laden season at Manchester United, a future away from England had suddenly become more attrac-tive. Despite Sir Alex Ferguson's stubborn reluctance to sell to Madrid – and he'd repeat the kerfuffle when Ramón Calderón came calling for Cristiano Ronaldo several years later – Beckham was eventually permitted to join the ranks of Madrid's superstars.

Yet even in this new city, the attention of the photographers never really let up, and the headlines roared on a near daily basis. Traditional media held sway, with the tabloid press wielding much of that power with scant regard for nuance or subtlety. The fact Beckham's wife Victoria was also a member of pop group The Spice Girls meant he featured as much on the news and entertainment pages as at the back of the book.

Twenty years on, the media landscape had changed so utterly that it's hard to quantify. There may no longer be gangs of paparazzi shadowing vehicles on mopeds, but the attention is, in its own way, even more relentlessly invasive. At night the Beckhams could lock the security gates and retreat within the walls of their luxury home to escape the prying eyes. Now, unwanted attention is just a click of a screen away, 24 hours a day, seven days a week. For young players desperate for their next fix of feedback, the smartphone is a piece of equipment as essential as shin pads or boots. Social media is an extension of the self, an essential part of the daily ritual in which everyone has a platform to showcase their very best version of themselves – and invite the world to comment in the process.

'That's an incredibly important thing to touch on,' says Lukas Jutkiewicz. 'Whether you are playing in La Liga or League Two there is still the opportunity to open yourself up for people to directly message you or share their feelings towards you. And you can see that instantly. I'm a little older and perhaps I don't value social media in the same way kids do. I didn't grow up with it and I would push my own son away from it. I don't think it's beneficial to open yourself up to the opinions of that many people – because your brain naturally gravitates towards the negative rather than the positive. I don't know how Jude deals with it. He has been so successful but there will still be people out there who try and push his buttons. It's another element of what young professionals have to deal with now. You get to that level and whether you like it or not you are a brand. So it would make sense for someone else to be taking care of that side of things.'

Still in his mid-thirties, coach Davide Ancelotti provides a generational bridge between his father Carlo and the Madrid players. Yet, despite his relative youth and in common with Jutkiewicz, Ancelotti Jnr has never caught the social media bug. Mindful and wary of the potential for unwanted and unhealthy levels of mental interference, he is no fan of the phenomenon. In days past there might have been a blanket ban on the use of phones within the confines of the training ground or stadium. Yet things have changed, and the balance of power has, for good or bad, swung towards players. At the very highest level there is a constant bargain between the bosses and players. The days of the autocratic outright control of a Ferguson or even a Fabio Capello are gone with managers having to be selective with their battles. Dependent on his players to buy into the team vision on the pitch, there are skirmishes that even Don Carlo might regard as not worth the fight. Especially when so many areas of player welfare, from nutrition to psychology are devolved to experts, not all of whom operate under the umbrella of the club.

'At the highest level today, players are advised by professionals,' explains Ancelotti Jnr. 'Each and every one of them has a psychologist and they are able to do it on their own. It's also true that the first feedback the players have after the game is from social media. Did I play well or not? The first answer is not from the coach. As soon as they come into the dressing room after the game, they open Instagram. They get the feedback from the people. It's not healthy. I don't have social media because I know that I can be affected by it. I don't like to read comments about my job so I don't have it. It's not mandatory to have it and a lot of the players do and they manage their accounts themselves. Maybe the oldest ones like Luka Modrić and Toni Kroos get other people to do it for them, but the young ones, you see them with Instagram all the time. They like to scroll and see videos and of course they will see comments which could affect them. It's something that could affect performance for sure. Regarding Jude, we've spoken to the club psychologist. He is prepared and of course his mother is in Madrid too.'

A tight support network is not only needed in the face of derision. It can also help stabilise the mind in the face of intense praise and adulation. Aside from the trophy lifts, there was a clutch of personal accolades to bejewel his debut season in Spain. First up came the Kopa Trophy, the junior version of the Ballon d'Or award that is presented in tandem with the game's most coveted non-team prize. Bellingham had finished runner-up to Barcelona's Pedri in 2021, midway through his second season in Germany, but for the 2023 ceremony at Paris's Théâtre du Châtelet, he was atop the podium. Awarded in recognition of his performances in his final year in Germany – and indeed for England at the 2022 World Cup in Qatar – Bellingham achieved some minor form of retribution for his Bundesliga heartache by nudging his old friend and former Bayern Munich rival Jamal Musiala into second place, with Pedri coming in third.

For the 21st edition of European football's Golden Boy award, awarded for performances across the calendar year of 2023, new ground was broken. The previous two decades had thrown up a colourful list of winners from the Netherlands' Rafael van der Vaart in 2003, through to Barcelona starlet Gavi in 2022. Initially established as a flagship prize by Italian sports news outlet *Tuttosport*, the prize has grown in prestige to become a truly trans-continental affair. From titles in Portugal (*A Bola*) through Germany (*Bild*) and Greece (*Ta Nea*), the award takes into account the opinion of 50 journalists across Europe. Of those canvassed, 45 placed Bellingham in first place, with the remaining five awarding him second place, giving him a record score of 485 out of 500. Musiala ranked second with 285 points, while the newly emergent Lamine Yamal netted 91 in third.

Less than 24 hours on from his near title-clinching April winner in El Clásico, it was time for the Laureus World Sport Awards which, conveniently, rolled into Madrid for its annual glitterfest. Decked out in a stylish dinner suit with eye-catching pin lapel and bell bottom trousers, Bellingham collected the World Breakthrough of the Year award from the previous winner, Spanish tennis star Carlos Alcaraz. There he mingled with the great and the good, and was snapped with Novak Djokovic, Jessica Ennis-Hill and

Usain Bolt among others. We've seen a plethora of celeb-rities mimic Bolt's signature victory pose, but this was an occasion for turning the tables. Rather than Bellingham extend his left arm and point skywards, the fastest sprinter of all time instead widened his stance in imitation of Bellingham's trademark goal celebration. It seemed like the world was flocking to Jude.

If Madrid hedged their bets slightly with his low-key presentation, a match day visit to the stadium leaves no doubt as to his hastily acquired hero status among the fol-lowers of Los Blancos. Two nights after parading the La Liga trophy at La Cibeles, Madrid were back in action for a league game against Alavés, a fixture that formed part of the build-up to the Champions League final. Climbing out of the Santiago Bernabéu metro station and looking up at the backs of the ascending pilgrims, it is instantly apparent that one number dominates all others. Bellingham 5 is now the most popular shirt in town and it's worn by supporters of all nationalities and genders on the concourses around the ground.

Shaun Singh, 35, is visiting from London and says: 'It is not easy to make the right decision in life, but he rejected a lot of top-flight football clubs in England in order to move to Dortmund from Birmingham. Not many players would have said no to Manchester United, but there's a passion for the sport and that's what makes me put his name on the back of my shirt. I don't know if there has been a more popular English player since Beckham, who was popular for different reasons. He was a fashion icon, a pop culture icon. Jude Bellingham is an icon for footballing reasons. The reward is the whole of Madrid wearing this shirt.

There's no Modrić. No Camavinga. No Vinicius Jr. It's all No. 5s. All Bellingham.'

Another of the hordes wearing the Bellingham motif is Samuel Millan, a 19-year-old student who has moved to Madrid from Venezuela. 'Jude is very sharp,' he remarks. 'He came in at 20 and straight away was a leader – that's not common at any club, far less Real Madrid. He's the ultimate professional, teammate and player. My football heroes were Cristiano and Benzema. Jude is similar in his attitude and the way he steps up when you need him. He could be here for ten years.'

Ryan Khoury, a Lebanese American who is in town to watch his first Madrid game, is also wearing five. 'I started watching Ricardo Kaká and then he moved to Madrid; after that Cristiano came and I fell in love with the club. All those stars left but here I am, still a fan. Bellingham is the new star. I just love how confident he is. I am in college but I am older than him. He is very inspiring.'

Freed up from the pressure of needing to win, Madrid turned on the style, with Bellingham claiming the first of his team's five goals with a beautifully angled left-foot volley. After pausing at the halfway line to take on his celebration stance, he is serenaded by the Madridistas, the coda to 'Hey Jude' ringing round the stadium like a hymn.

Certainly until England's latest summer of not quite managing to bring football 'home', direct criticism of Bellingham had been hard to source. And, without exception, everyone who agreed to cooperate in the research for this book spoke only of their admiration of not only his sporting acumen but the roundness and maturity of his character. Yet Jude has said enough in public to let it be known that he is sensitive to criticism. And that he uses it to spur himself on to greater things. Yet if the perceived slights continue – and they will, sometimes unfairly – he will need to develop a mechanism for blocking it out. If he's not likely to grow a thicker skin, then an efficient filtration device will be required instead.

There is already plenty evidence to suggest that although he is very much a product of his times, he is in possession of the human and emotional skills necessary to navigate this tech-heavy world. Kevin Betsy made Jude an England captain at under-15 level precisely because of his interpersonal skills. 'We did various studies,' revealed Betsy. 'One point was on youth leadership. Young players do not communicate well with each other, and they spend a lot of time on the phone. But Jude could hold his own, at 13, with players older than him in those situations. He was very mature mentally. Mark Bellingham raised two fantastic youngsters in Jude and Jobe. Jude is a guy whom you would invite over to your house to meet your family and have dinner. He is the son you would love to have. He has perfect manners, respect for everyone . . . he is exemplary. Jude would make sure his teammates were punctual, he picked up litter in the locker room when we played away from home. He made sure everything was clean. He was one of the leaders to ensure that things were done correctly. You could trust him in any aspect.'

Perhaps the first high-profile example of Jude's social conscience came at the conclusion of the Covid-delayed Euro 2020 finals. Just 17 years of age when the tournament kicked off in the summer of 2021, Jude was a squad player for the summer, but stepped up forcefully when a quite ugly backlash descended on certain members of the team following the penalty shoot-out defeat to Italy in the final. Bukayo Saka, Jadon Sancho and Marcus Rashford received racial abuse in the wake of the defeat, and, in response, Jude tweeted an image of his three teammates wearing crowns, alongside a message of support: 'So proud to have teammates with such top character. Takes huge bollocks just to volunteer. As for the racism, hurtful but not surprising. Will never get bored of saying that more needs to be done. Educate and control the platforms!'

A year later, in an interview with CNN's Darren Lewis, he expanded on the episode, drawing on his own experiences of racist abuse: 'It felt like the country had united and we were all on the same path. We had black players in the team, players of all different backgrounds in the team. And then as soon as they missed the penalty, they're not English they're just black.' He continued: 'My mum, my dad are two huge role models of mine because of the way they have carried themselves and the things they have had to face in their own journeys. Especially my mum. She is always giving me a lot of lessons in how I will be perceived by other people. Sometimes because of the colour of my skin. Sometimes we are stereotyped. I talk about my football heroes, I talk about Gerrard, I talk about Rooney and I talk about Zidane. But I've got a black woman that I live with every day and I see the way she carries herself and for me you couldn't have a bigger hero. I say to my mum quite often that after a majority of games I will get a racist message in my Instagram inbox. Whether it's one, two or three can depend on what I have done in the game. There is not a single job in the world where you deserve to be criticised with racism. But that's the world we live in. That's why we have got to do more. That's why the people in power have got to do more.'

Bellingham's power to effect change from a regulatory point of view is minimal, but he has been determined to keep up his end of the bargain. One suspects his teammates will be glad of the solidarity. In June 2024, three men were sentenced to eight months in jail for racially abusing Vinicius at a La Liga match, the first convictions of their kind in a Spanish court. His parents have been careful to shield him from the media spotlight, but on the occasion of Madrid's arrival in England for their Champions League quarter-final against Manchester City, Jude was the designated player chosen by Madrid to represent the club at the pre-match press conference. Naturally, the ice was broken with a few platitudes about how good it was to be back in England. But it wasn't all softballs and underhand serves.

The previous Sunday his teammate Aurélien Tchouaméni had been subjected to an alleged racial gesture in a La Liga match away to Real Mallorca. Asked about the matter, Bellingham spoke with force and clarity and the Spanish football authorities were in his crosshairs. He said: 'I think in the games where we go away, in La Liga especially, you almost get used to that. I wasn't even aware of the Tchouaméni incident. I think that's a massive problem in itself. More has got to be done, whether it's punishment or how you react to it. It's a horrible way for a player to prepare for a game, knowing they're probably going to get racially abused. It's disgusting. It shouldn't happen. The people in power need to do more. No one deserves that kind of thing. It's a call-out for people in charge. It's going to be something I imagine we just have to deal with. You just have to play your game and hope people look after you.'

Madrid's PR department won't necessarily have expected such a lengthy answer, but nor could they have any qualms with the content or delivery of the player's words. 'He is a very intelligent bloke,' says Jutkiewicz. 'He's talking the other week about Vinicius and some of the abuse he has to suffer. He doesn't seem to shy away from that. That just shows the maturity. You forget how young he is. It's a lot to deal with, all that pressure on your shoulders. Say the wrong thing at the wrong moment. He seems to have escaped that so far which is impressive in itself. Because he engages. He doesn't do non-answers.'

There was that incident in Germany where Bellingham's emotions in the aftermath of a defeat to Bayern Munich saw him publicly question the integrity of a referee. There was a financial punishment for that indiscretion but more importantly a lesson learned – even if he might reasonably have argued that he didn't actually say anything that wasn't already a matter of public record. Paul Lambert winced at that criticism of Felix Zwayer, and his prior involvement in a German match-fixing scandal. 'Do you know what? That's something a young person would do. If Mats Hummels or Marco Reus had been asked the same question, they'd have batted it away. But right after the game, a young player's emotions swirling, the words are out before you know it. Everybody is entitled to their voice and their principles, but you don't want that to spill into crazy things. The heat of battle is incredible. Anything can happen in football; someone can wind you up and you think you've had enough. In my day that could happen in the tunnel. I saw fights. Now it's virtually impossible. Players can't even speak on the pitch; they talk with their hands over their mouths. Then you get the thing now: "Lip reader says Jude Bellingham said . . ." He'll learn as he gets older.'

A lip reader was indeed deployed to investigate another contentious moment involving Bellingham during his first season of Spanish football, and so it's tricky to pin down the specifics of his contretemps with Mason Greenwood during a La Liga fixture against Getafe. Getafe had signed Greenwood at the start of the season following his ostracism at Manchester United in the wake of a six-month internal investigation, which was launched after charges against the player, including attempted rape and assault, were dropped. Greenwood had debuted for United at 17 and played over 100 times for the club before he was arrested in January 2022 following allegations surrounding material that had been placed online. He was subsequently charged with attempted rape, coercive behaviour and assault occasioning actual bodily harm. The charges were dropped in February 2023 after key witnesses withdrew. At the conclusion of the investigation, United had confirmed that Greenwood would leave the club by mutual consent, but that they would 'offer its support to Mason and his family during this period of transition'.

Matters blew up when Bellingham tackled Greenwood near the touchline and, in the immediate aftermath, made a comment in the direction of his compatriot. The moment caused some consternation in the Spanish media and, at the behest of La Liga, an investigation was launched by the Spanish FA, amid allegations that Bellingham had used the word 'rapist'. According to *Marca*, a lip reader was drafted in to determine whether he had actually used the word 'rubbish'. Perhaps appropriately, the matter disappeared weeks later when it was determined that there was no credible evidence to proceed.

Bellingham likes to play on the edge. And it's clearly not in his character to stay silent in the face of perceived injustice or to back down when he feels to have personally been wronged. Those two elements were conflated on the occasion of his first red card in Spain, a punishment meted out by referee Gil Manzano after his reaction to the disallowed goal against Valencia. The Spanish FA decided that particular outburst contained more than enough weight to merit censure and handed down a two-game ban. Despite Bellingham's subsequent claim that he was being made an example of, his manager felt the need to intervene and implore the player to modify his behaviour in future.

Neither Carlo nor Davide Ancelotti want Bellingham to lose the fire that burns within, but it must be tempered. 'It's difficult to find something that Jude does not do well,' says Davide Ancelotti. 'But the thing he can improve is that sometimes he loses focus on the game by talking to referees. He trash talks with the opponents a lot which is something that athletes do and sometimes it can help. A lot of players do it. I think it's a weapon for a player to trash talk sometimes. Because it is allowed. But you don't have to say anything to the referees, even though he becomes upset and frustrated a lot. It's true that sometimes he loses the plot. That's normal when you are competitive but he needs to find the balance. When he scored in Valencia he got a red card. So his attitude with the referees has to change. But we also have Vinicius who is worse . . .'

Lambert believes time will smooth off the rougher edges around Bellingham's game. 'He got sent off against Valencia because the referee blew the whistle – that's just frustration. I don't think there's malice there. I don't think there's any craziness to him. If he commits a foul it's a genuine mistimer. He doesn't go in to do anyone. I don't think you can totally take the edge away from him. You'd maybe lose a little. As he gets older he'll manage that himself, know when to stay away from it. Curtail it. I remember playing for St Mirren v Celtic growing up. There was a fracas on the pitch and I was involved and the great Tommy Burns, who was on the other side and never knew who I was at that point, came over and said: "Wee man, just leave it. Let all the nutters deal with it." I've never forgotten that. I was probably as young as Jude and I wanted to get in there. Jude will become that older player and he'll look after the young ones. And in the meantime he has a brilliant manager in Carlo to look after him. As long as the hunger is still there. By all accounts he has a girlfriend which is great – as long as it doesn't give him the distraction of clubbing and all that.'

While Beckham and Victoria courted the media and even sold the rights to their wedding to *Hello!* magazine, Bellingham has done a remarkably good job of keeping details of his personal life under wraps. He's been linked with a handful of women, most consistently Dutch model Laura Celia Valk, but while both she and Jude are prolific on social media, each has remained silent on any ongoing romance, real or otherwise. Any future relationship might, naturally, affect the dynamic of his inner circle and it's feasible that over time the influence of his parents could lessen. On all available evidence it's hard to see him losing focus.

For journalist Graham Hunter, the arrival of Jude Bellingham not only added an exciting talent to the Spanish fray but also a fresh and thoughtful new voice. He explains: 'Having met Jude twice and listened to him every time he has spoken out, I think he is an exceptional representative for the sport we love. I could listen to him endlessly and I can't wait for the time when he will choose, perhaps only when captain of England, to have more contact with the media. He may do that under his own set of controls so that he can bring the quality of thinking, the quality of articulacy and quality of message that I know he possesses. I find him bright. I think he comes from an intelligent, forthright and principled background. I don't know the family intimately by any stretch of the imagination, but I watch how they have protected and yet grown two talented sons. During his first year at Dortmund I first became aware that his mum was like a *consigliere*, something of a body-guard around him. I thought that was shrewd. When some players have their parents involved, it will often be because the parent is scared of letting go of control. Sometimes you see them involved because they are greedy and they want the marketing side of things to be under their control. But when I have watched Jude's parents' respective involve-ments, I've seen evidence of what they thought their sons could turn out to be. I appreciate sportsmen and women who are forthright and self-confident and feel they can take on the world and win.'

A human resources professional by trade, Denise has indeed taken over the role of Jude's chief of staff and is acknowledged to have her hand on both his financial and media affairs. Yet as Jude has let slip, she also plays the more fundamental and ultimately important role of mum. As he prepared to collect his Kopa Trophy, Real Madrid issued a video clip of Denise helping their new young recruit into his flared Louis Vuitton suit. As she performed the tricky act of fixing his bow tie, Jude was heard to remark, 'All them people are so mature, I can't even get changed on my own. My life is a lie!'

The handsomely paid stars of the Madrid dressing room are, generally, housed between two distinct yet abundantly well-heeled residential districts in the city. To the west of the city centre sits La Finca, yet Jude – and Denise – have chosen the more northerly La Moraleja as their base, a quieter neighbourhood yet one that grants better proximity to the training ground on the eastern outskirts of the capital. He won't go short of fine dining options in La Moraleja, but the decision to prioritise work when choosing accommodation speaks to that careful family strategy we have heard so much about.

'I believe both his parents have patently, evidently, taught him how to live, how to develop and how to play the game,' continues Hunter. 'Unless you are an outright genius that's really important. I don't think Jude is Messi, but I do think he is exceptional and you don't get to be like him unless you are taught well. I think he has been taught about values, about maturity, how to handle fame and adulation. So all in all if I met a 20-year-old achieving a tenth of what he is achieving, I would already be full of admiration. To have him in the running for a Ballon d'Or and be spoken of as a future or imminent England captain.

Having been essential to Madrid winning the Champions League. At 20 to be seeing the tip of the iceberg . . . I haven't seen this many times in my life.'

He may enjoy a life of luxury in La Moraleja and reap the trappings of advertising deals with Adidas, Lucozade, Gucci and Kim Kardashian's new underwear brand Skims, but Jude has patently remained close and true to his roots. Back in those days when he was earning his £145 a week at Birmingham, he began – at the behest of his father – to support The Mustard Seed Project, which provides education, healthcare and food for underprivileged children in Kenya. He remains supportive of the Miche Bora Nursery and Primary School, helping with fundraising initiatives in addition to his own personal donations.

He may have closed out his Birmingham City career in empty stadiums, but in his final interview for the club's in-house channel he made a point of referring to his interactions with the club's fans, of 'bridging a gap' when he left. Having grown up a supporter it's something that has remained evidently important to him and never more obvious than through the relationship he has established with one Blues supporter. Lynda Courts caught the bug for football travel in the wake of City's Carling Cup win in 2011 and subsequent brief adventures in European football. When these continental trips dried up, she and her family resolved to start following the English national team and have done so carrying a St George's flag bearing the legend of Redditch Blues, named after their home town, just south of the city. As soon as the turnstiles open, the flag is placed behind the goal and Lynda waits for the players to emerge for their pre-match walk round. 'The first time

I waved this flag at Jude, he spotted it and waved to me,' she says. 'I waved back and it became a tradition. Whether it was home or away I would get in as soon as I could, put the big flag up and then stand waiting for him to wave to me. I don't think he really knew who he was waving at, but then it started happening at the end of games too. Our group would wave the flag and he'd wave back at us. Like a conversation.'

The dialogue intensified at a World Cup qualifier in San Marino, a 10-0 victory. 'There was a big Perspex barrier which must have been about seven foot high,' recalls Lynda. 'As they were warming up, I stood and held the flag up as usual and he signalled to me. I jokingly shouted: "Can I have your shirt, Jude?" He did a thumbs up. After the game, Jude headed straight towards me. There was this big guy to the left of me. Jude had to get the shirt over the Perspex and I thought there's no way I'm getting to that first. Jude literally pointed at me and the guy caught the shirt and gave it to me. I was virtually in tears. I tell you it smelled of his aftershave. He'd played 90 minutes but that was the scent. We got back to the hotel room and had a proper look. It had a grass stain from him doing a slide tackle and I promised I was never going to wash it.'

Lynda later had the shirt signed at a sponsors' event in Birmingham and has watched in admiration as its former wearer has grown in stature. 'All Bluenoses are proud of the fact he was made in Brum and I don't think he is going to forget those roots. At the very start of his interview right after the Champions League final, he said, "As you go through life," which are also the first words of our anthem 'Keep Right On'. Whether it was intentional or not, every

Birmingham City fan will have heard that and made the connection. The new owners want Birmingham to be as big as Man City. If that happens and Jude decides to leave Real Madrid, I think he will come back. It might be towards the end of his career, but I really do think he will come back to wear that No. 22 shirt in the Champions League.'

Blues fans are entitled to dream, but they could be waiting a long time for that sort of homecoming. If Jude makes good on his ambition to remain with Madrid for the next decade and a half, he may never play in English club football again. And if he is to enjoy that kind of longevity, he may need to find an accommodation with both club and country to reduce the unprecedented strain that is already being placed upon his young body.

Chapter 12

DON'T CARRY THE WORLD
UPON YOUR SHOULDERS

IN ONE of his very earliest conversations with Jude, Carlo
Ancelotti made one solemn request of his new signing:
'Please tell me if you are tired.' The Italian had marvelled at
the numbers posted by Bellingham since his breakthrough
year at Birmingham. Forty-four appearances in that debut
campaign. A further 46 in his first year at Dortmund, a
level he maintained through seasons two and three. And
now, having watched him hold his own in his squad's
ever-intensifying training sessions ahead of the new campaign, the coach knew he had an elite level athlete on his
hands. And one that was bowling over his new teammates
with the skill and personality he brought to every practice
routine he completed. Yet there was a certain caution in
the coach's mind. Ancelotti may have seen and done it all,
but even he couldn't know for certain what the long-term
effects such a ferocious workload might have on a young
player's body. Or indeed his mind. As with most matters,
Ancelotti decided to manage the matter intuitively.

A lovely story developed late in the La Liga season,
just as Madrid were preparing to take their victory lap

after seeing off Barça in the decisive second Clásico of the season. There's a convention in Spanish football, one that seems refreshingly open when compared to the suspicious and paranoid machinations of the British game, by which football clubs routinely name match-day squads ahead of the next fixture. The practice allows media pundits and commentators to prepare more precisely and keeps fans in the loop regarding the health and fitness of their favourite players. For Madrid's next game, a La Liga trip to San Sebastián to face Real Sociedad on a Friday night, the list dropped minus one notable name. Gastroenteritis had laid Bellingham low in the wake of the Laureus Awards – one wouldn't like to speculate on the quality of the canapés on offer at the Palacio de Cibeles – but come the morning of the game, as the team reported in to prepare for their flight to the Basque Country, Bellingham arrived sharp, imploring Ancelotti to include him in the travelling party. With a huge Champions League semi-final around the corner, the Italian was sceptical but relented and a plane ticket was allocated in Bellingham's name. He travelled, was named among the substitutes and remained on the bench as a much-changed team secured a 1-0 victory. It was another canny piece of man management from the coach, allowing the player's enthusiasm to prevail just far enough, only to provide a gentle check at the vital moment. No doubt Jude would have happily bounded out on to the pitch that night and he might not have been any the worse for it.

Yet there is an unknowable element to his ever-questing desire to push himself. Just how much top-level football is it possible to cram into a young player's mind and body without causing an adverse effect? Madrid's Valdebebas complex has all the latest monitoring equipment and a team of sports scientists, chefs and dieticians to keep the players nourished and healthy. Yet the human body remains a fragile thing, one at the mercy of a high-speed game in which honed specimens of bone, blood and muscle compete in a high-stakes contact sport.

The dangers were laid bare in the days leading up to the Champions League final when FIFPRO, effectively the worldwide union for professional footballers, produced its annual report, a document focused heavily on the issue of player workload and written in an alarming tone. Boasting a membership of 65,000 pooled from 66 national associations, FIFPRO have long been concerned that commercial concerns take priority over the welfare of those employed to play the game. At the heart of the report was a section devoted exclusively to Bellingham and drew a direct comparison with ten high-profile and prodigious English young players from the last 20 years.

The data made for stark and surprising reading. Before his 20th birthday in June 2023, Bellingham had clocked up 14,445 minutes of first-team football for clubs and country. By the same age, Wayne Rooney, his nearest 'challenger', had managed just 10,989. Michael Owen, commonly reckoned to have burnt out by his late twenties, was third with 9,187. The remaining seven had registered less than half of Jude's first-team minutes, with the bottom two – David Beckham and Steven Gerrard – showing just 829 and 2,853 respectively. The sample may have leant towards the so-called Golden Generation, but it also took in Harry Kane (4,010) and close contemporary Jadon Sancho, who had acquired only 7,106 by the time he reached the same milestone in 2020.

Darren Burgess, a former director of performance at Arsenal and currently a consultant for FIFPRO, helped put the study together. He says: 'We don't really know the limits that a player has, but what we do know is that Bellingham is going into new territory. We haven't seen this before. Nobody has done what he has done in terms of senior minutes. Some might say, "Well, he is paid well, and living his dream," and that's absolutely true, but we don't know the effect of playing six times more minutes than David Beckham at his age, which is quite scary really. We just don't know whether he will get overloaded or whether he already is. Some might say his performances at the Euros were a bit flat, but there's no way to really judge that. We just have to see where he ends up over the next couple of years.'

Back in that Birmingham year, Pep Clotet was acutely aware of the potential of overloading Jude's still developing young body in the energy-sapping slog of a Championship season. 'He had a crash course on the physical side of the game with us,' says Clotet. 'I remember looking at him after every league game and he looked absolutely exhausted! It was very demanding. The Championship is more unpredictable than most leagues. Games swing from one team to the other and there are more mistakes than elsewhere. This puts more physical pressure on the players. I remember one day I wanted to leave him out of an FA Cup game against Leicester because he had a niggle. He was trying to argue but I told him I was going to insist. He was only 16 so it was important to let him rest well. I think the pandemic helped some teams – it helped Leeds massively to get promoted because of the type of game they played. And it helped Jude to recover perfectly, rest and go again.'

By the time he reached the end of his first season in Spain, Bellingham did seem to be running on fumes. In the 70th minute of Madrid's Champions League win over Dortmund, he took a moment to lean on one of Wembley's goalposts and stretch out his calf, a sure sign of fatigue. Towards the end of the domestic season he'd missed matches with an ankle problem and on the eve of the final he'd been pictured with a strapping on his shoulder. The shoulder problem surfaced via a dislocation suffered in a match against Rayo Vallecano on 5 November, causing him to miss subsequent games against Braga and Valencia. After his return to the side, Ancelotti admitted the midfielder was having to undertake specific work to strengthen the joint which was still not fully healed. Pointedly he ruled out surgery in the short term and insisted that Bellingham would improve every day going forward.

If strapping remained essential so late in the season and indeed throughout the Euros, then it's not unreasonable to assume that a procedure might be required to preserve its long-term health. If corrective surgery is required, when might such a procedure be scheduled? So key was Bellingham to this Benzema-less Madrid that a mid-season break of up to two months was inconceivable. Going into the summer as favourites for the Euros, England would hardly have been keen to see their stand-out creator miss out. And Jude himself has proved repeatedly that he is loath to take any kind of break, to sit out even a routine league match when there is something tangible to play for. Of course, Bellingham's shoulder *might* just clear up in its own good time, but the stakes are so high in football that straightforward doctor's orders are no longer the primary factor in such decisions.

In the days after facing Slovenia in England's third group fixture at the Euros, Bellingham confessed to feeling 'absolutely dead' at the end of the match. 'When you are walking off the pitch and have given everything, you feel in a certain way, physically and emotionally,' responded Southgate when asked about the comment. 'Jude missed a period at the end of the season with an ankle injury so he will have benefited from the matches he has had. Of course . . . freshness might make a difference in the latest stages of matches. But I am not concerned about Jude Bellingham.'

Not only did Bellingham last the 90 minutes against Slovakia in England's next match, but he produced that outrageous overhead kick deep in stoppage time to keep England in the tournament. So much for absolute death. But there were clear signs that Bellingham was only really playing in bursts, his body straining to keep up with the demands of the game and his own mind. The contrast with his performances in Qatar, a winter World Cup tournament which brought the world's best together in their mid-season pomp, was stark.

'The player obviously wants to play in all the games and why wouldn't you at that level?' adds Burgess. 'Most managers are only five games away from being sacked so it's not so often that they'll feel comfortable resting their best players. The only safe or objective way we can do this is by adjusting the calendar to take it out of the manager's and the player's hands. That's kind of what we are suggesting and even what the players themselves are suggesting. We did a survey of 90-odd high performance managers working across the world and asked these university-trained fitness experts what the optimum number of games was.

The answer was around the 50-game mark. So it's not about playing significantly fewer games. Players in Spain and Europe are going to play that anyway, but we don't want to overload them.'

On 13 June 2024, the day before the Euros started, FIFPRO followed up their annual report by lodging a lawsuit against FIFA. A little over a month later, it was revealed that they had garnered widespread club support as they filed a complaint to the European Commission regarding the international match calendar. Joined by the European Leagues body, drawn from 33 countries, and also La Liga who sit independently of the EL, FIFPRO released a statement accusing FIFA of an 'abuse of dominance'. Among their key issues was the introduction of the new 32-team Club World Cup, scheduled to kick off in 2025, and FIFA's failure to grant a mandatory 28-day rest period between seasons.

No club is likely to feel this load more than Madrid. The 2024–25 campaign was set to pitch Los Blancos into seven distinct competitions with a potential for 72 games in 11 months. An expanded Champions League, the revival of the Intercontinental Cup and the Club World Cup are all in the mix for what seems like an impossible schedule. Intriguingly, Ancelotti had initially appeared to rail against the latter tournament. In an interview with Italian title *Il Giornale* in June 2024, he was quoted as saying: 'FIFA can forget it; footballers and clubs will not participate in that tournament. Like us, other clubs will refuse the invitation.' And yet Madrid quickly rushed out a retraction of Ancelotti's words, assuring everyone that they would indeed be taking part and that the coach, for his part, had been taken out of context.

By wandering off message, Ancelotti merely confirmed the view of most sensible coaches, that profit is being placed before player wellbeing. Burgess believes a tipping point has been reached. 'There is enough noise about it and not just from player unions but players and coaches themselves,' he argues. 'Enough people are now saying we can't sustain this. You read quotes from players saying they're only at 70 per cent. The Norwegian player Fredrik Aursnes at Benfica has retired from international football because he played 66 games last season. We don't want to see players pacing – going at half or three-quarter pace. We want to see your Bellinghams play at top speed and top pace. But eventually there is going to be a breaking point if we keep going the way we are. With Bellingham what we are essentially saying is that we are getting into unknown territory; it's so different to anything we have seen in the past. I've been with club managers who say they used to play 60 games a season, but the game just wasn't as quick. Look at the old footage – it's a completely different game. Fortunately, Bellingham plays in Spain where the league is a little bit less consistently intense. That's objectively shown by the stats and the stadium tracking data.'

Clotet would agree that Jude has landed in the league which will give him the best chance of protecting and insuring his condition for the long term. While Madrid may have a fixture load like few other clubs, Clotet reasons that the style of football is not as physically punishing as that practised, for example, in England's second tier. 'Unfortunately, footballers play so many games, especially in a club like Real Madrid where they fight for so many competitions and where every player is an international,' he continues. 'There is stress, and everybody responds differently to that. It's hard to keep that constant focus on giving your maximum, which to be fair, Jude does. The good thing for him is that physically the Spanish league is very different to some others. You have many strong, world-famous players who have made themselves in the Spanish league. Some are still playing and they have been helped by the level of focus on the physical side of the game. Since the 1990s, Spain has offered studies at university on how to become a physical trainer for any sport. So we have a long history now, around 30 years, of producing professionals who have studied just to do this job. Then there's the tactical side. The level of the coaching education in Spain and the culture is based on how to be as organised as possible without sacrificing the beauty of the game. Some countries make those sacrifices and try to be over-organised. Think about typical Italian football where the tactical element, especially defensive, is very important. In Spain it's about the whole team, attack and defend to be as good as possible, but also economical. That helps too.'

For some players – Lionel Messi being the prime example – there are ways to adapt to the schedule through economy of movement. Famous for strolling around the pitch waiting and scanning for his next opportunity, the Argentinian was a master at conserving energy. Bellingham's game, his mentality and his position on the field does not allow for such inertia. He has to be dynamic and his natural movement draws physical attention from opponents. 'You can't expect Jude Bellingham to take a game off,' concludes Burgess. 'Forcing that through extended off-season and mid-season breaks, specified FIFA windows, is probably the only way we can protect Bellingham from himself.'

*

The risk of physical burnout is just one of the challenges facing Bellingham as he seeks to build on his impressive first year in Spain. After such a scintillating debut, a recalibration is likely, both in terms of his role and how he is viewed by the wider fan base. He no longer carries the element of surprise. Nor is he either the bright young thing or the shiny new signing at Madrid. If all eyes have been drawn to 2024's marquee signing Kylian Mbappé, there are also plenty keeping a lookout for his striking understudy, the 18-year-old Brazilian Endrick. With those two added to the attack, there will be more opportunities for Bellingham to revert to his natural midfield role yet perhaps fewer occasions on which to strike up his favourite Messianic pose.

There was once a time when a young adult was said to come of age on their 21st birthday. Yet for Bellingham, who'd already scaled most of football's big mountains before reaching that milestone, the big challenge will be to sustain not only football excellence but mental equilibrium. Chastened yet wily opponents taken aback by the impudence and nerve of last season's rising star will be out to restore some pride if not settle a score.

Ramón Calderón has seen it all before, but does admit to being taken aback by just how well Bellingham adapted as a 20-year-old newcomer. 'I think we learned a very good lesson with the Galacticos,' says the former president. 'It was incredible for our reputation, image and prestige to have Figo, Zidane, Ronaldo, Beckham, Roberto Carlos, Iker Casillas, Guti, Sergio Ramos and so on. But some players were doing commercials more than they were working on the training ground. We forgot what is really important in life which is to be focused on hard work, perseverance and sacrifice. We knew Bellingham was a very good player, but his performances have been above expectations. He was the main scorer in his first year. I think this is a story that is very difficult to understand. I mean we are talking about Real Madrid.

'For me, Mbappé is the best player we can have. He reminds me of Ronaldo the Brazilian. Really strong, fast and he can score easily at any moment. I don't know his character but I know Ancelotti is the right manager. Ancelotti, (Vicente) Del Bosque and Zidane have been the coaches that a club like Real Madrid needs. They have been able to combine talent with motivation, to make players feel free even though tactically they are very good. It does not work properly when you have coaches who are rigid and strict. Mourinho for example. A good coach but always the protagonist. And when the team lost, coaches like him were always blaming others – the referees, UEFA, FIFA, UNICEF . . . it's true! So you have to be humble. The best coaches admit "it was my fault" and the players receive that message in a very good way.'

Bellingham proved so flexible that he was utilised in a range of roles, often sacrificing his own enjoyment for the task at hand. Davide Ancelotti recalls a frank conversation, instigated by his father, after Madrid's Champions League win in Manchester. 'I think what's impressed my father is the humility Jude has,' he explains. 'For example, we played him as a striker for some games and the team was winning, but he wasn't performing like he had in the rest of the season. Because it was working he was afraid to tell us – he didn't feel comfortable because he didn't want to affect the team. And because he struggled to tell us we had to take it out of him. Jude is a superstar of England, but that example shows he is really humble. And it's better to be too humble than to be too far the other way. For him that was a good learning point. My father told him: "You need to tell the manager how you feel and what you think." He understood why we put him there tactically and he put the team first. He played well but I think he is right – he plays better on the left where he can see the game from behind. He likes to take the ball from the defenders and watch the picture from another perspective. As a striker he sometimes has the ball behind him.'

In this regard, Ancelotti expects the team's new range of attacking options to aid Bellingham: 'I don't think playing with a No. 9 would affect Jude's performance, it could help. In his first season we did sometimes play with him behind a striker. He can perfectly play as a No. 10. I think it's even better to have a striker to pin the centre-halves for him because then he can come from behind.'

Comparisons are inevitable but not necessarily helpful. Bellingham has some of Zidane's elegance, but the Frenchman's snake-hipped ability to contort and bend the very direction of a game in a single movement remains unmatched. Jude can dribble too, just not quite with the devilment of a Maradona or a Messi. He has power and goalscoring form but you wouldn't call him another Cristiano. Yet it's rare to find a player with such a broad skill set. It's not inconceivable that he could slot into any outfield position and excel in the assigned role.

'Jude obviously likes to be the protagonist,' says Guillem Balague. 'He doesn't hide. Sometimes you see him trying too hard because he wants to be the guy that sorts things out, but at Real Madrid he won't need to do that so often. In the second part of the season he wasn't perfect. There were different reasons for that, one being the adaptability of Spanish players, who learned to defend better against his threat. Also his position changed so that he had to defend more and help Vinicius or Rodrygo. I'm sure that was frustrating to him because he could not attack the spaces in the same way. But already in 12 months he has had to adapt from being the superstar that saves the team to being a help to others. Not bad for a first season.'

What truly sets Jude apart is his precocity of character. There have been plenty of boy wonders arrive to set the game alight, but few have managed it with the forcefulness of Bellingham. He has the capacity to win a match on his own. But when the chips are down you can bet your life he'll be the one bending the ear of each and every team-mate around him to make something happen. He'll lead by example but won't allow a colleague to get away with a lazy day. And when he arrived to a dressing room still smarting from a bruising end to the previous season, it was he who provided the drive and the impetus to get off the canvas and fight anew.

'He came into such a coruscating environment and instantly made everyone sit up, instantly had the senior players hinting to their entourages and the media that somebody special had arrived,' says Graham Hunter. 'In the very first La Liga television programme of last season that I appeared on, they asked me about Bellingham and I said: "A phenomenon has arrived." I think that has been proven accurate as a word. He has superseded even my expectations for the season, but it's easier now in retrospect to look at the trophies and the stats and the celebration and the brilliance of how he shines when he speaks to the media, the fact he has learned Spanish. Also the fact he helped England to a final! It's much easier with retrovision to speak well of him. But what also struck me was not just his level of talent. Not everyone has commented on how ready he was. Not how physically impressive or how impressive his scoring or leadership record is. How ready he was. The readiness for the elevation in quality and demands of whom he was going to train with. And the readiness for what the club was going to be like compared to Dortmund. It's extraordinary. I think that has been obscured by what has subsequently been achieved.'

And perhaps what he has achieved was, temporarily at least, itself obscured by the reaction to England's ails at Euro 2024. It would be wrong to suggest that Jude was cast as a scapegoat for the team's failure to win the tournament, but in the search to find reasons for the team's lack of fluency and failure to beat Spain at the final hurdle, focus inevitably fell on to the biggest personality in the team. Bellingham's media profile has been carefully curated, often at the behest of his family, to hand-picked interviews and post-match appearances with broadcast rights holders. At the end of these brief, soft-batted encounters, the presenters and panellists often gush at how mature the young man is. In some aspects that maturity is overstated. There are plenty of 17- and 18-year-olds up and down the country who up sticks and leave home and find a way to cook and launder for themselves without the obvious and spectacular advantages of a professional footballer's salary and support network.

Those journalists asked to cover the England squad at Euro 2024 were quite entitled to ask why Bellingham should be excused his place on the rota for press conferences, especially given his place on Southgate's leadership council. And it won't just be the men and women of the media whose noses will have been placed out of joint. One wonders what the likes of Harry Kane, Declan Rice and Jordan Pickford – each of whom regularly fronted up – felt of the Bellingham exemption.

Yet it's also important to cut the young man some slack. His reaction to defeat in the final of Euro 2024 *was* a bit like a teenage tantrum; that kick at the drinks carton a match-day equivalent of a door slammed at the downright unfairness of it all. Yet after regaining his composure, Bellingham did make a point of going round each and every one of his teammates to offer his support. Various post-mortem opinion pieces alluded to disharmony within the squad, referring back to that Adidas advert and the cold reaction of his teammates as he shook their hands in the Berlin aftermath. Yet what were people expecting – three cheers and high-fives all round? It was perhaps more instructive to look at the reaction of the Spanish players, of opponents on the night but colleagues who worked day in, day out with him during the season like Nacho, Joselu and Dani Carvajal who all took the time to console their younger counterpart. Long after the medals had been distributed at the Olympic Stadium, Bellingham was to be found sitting with Carvajal and his children.

So what if there is a belligerent streak to his character. It's those complexities and contradictions that make him so interesting. They also render him human. The move to Germany was clever in that it allowed him to grow up away from the glare of the English media, but international duty brings him into the eyeline of the pundits and opinion-formers. And a deep run at a major tournament means there's six weeks of analysis to absorb. 'Criticism from your own country is different,' says journalist Jonathan Northcroft. 'And it depends where it goes. But let's have some perspective – we are not talking about David Beckham having effigies burned outside the house. We are not talking about Wayne Rooney being the focus of the world's attention. So the backlash Jude has suffered is not that bad in the context of previous stuff. But he is clearly sensitive to any criticism. You saw it in that interview after the Champions League final when he said he'd shown his doubters . . . you've never had any doubters, Jude, what are you talking about?! There might have been a primary school teacher who told him to focus on his maths and play less football, but there won't be many others ready to crawl out of the woodwork saying they'd doubted him. Clearly, any slight or insult will resonate with him. Let's not over-dramatise but I'm predicting this will grow and it will be different territory for him. It will be interesting to see how he reacts. But I would expect him to use it as fuel because that's what his personality seems to be all about. It's about using any little slight as power.'

Days after Euro 2024, Gareth Southgate resigned as national coach, meaning it will fall to someone new to try and take the final step with England. His successor will need to decide whether to continue to trying to shoehorn all the squad's best players into the side. Or, with Harry Kane now the other side of 30 and showing the first signs of weariness at the Euros, he may instead take the decision to build a side round Bellingham. It's a problem that does not exist at Madrid, a club that demands big personality if not arrogance in its first-team stars. The Ancelottis may have harboured the standard reservations around Bellingham's readiness to play for Madrid, but those fears dissipated as soon as they saw him at work. Rewarded with those new contracts they may even have come to feel gratitude for the arrival of the Golden Boy.

'The only doubt we had at the start was how he was going to fit in Madrid as an English player, says Davide. 'We knew his character, that he was really mature, but not *so* much! When you talk to Jude it's like speaking to a 30-year-old man. He copes very well with the expectations and with the pressure that we have here. The fact he started so well only increased those expectations, but he is able to cope with that. Jude is really ambitious. He is always thinking about the future and he is really focused. He has a clear voice. But he is really humble too. He has no ego. He is a team player. I don't know if he is able to stay like this. I think he has the strength to stay humble for his whole career, just like Luka Modrić has. Modrić is 39 but he has no ego. Let's see in the future if he is able to keep the humility that he has right now. After that the main challenge is just to try and be consistent, to repeat the performances he showed in the first season. I've seen players with a full belly. They have achieved so much and then they rely only on technical ability. The best players here in the past were those who achieved consistency. Cristiano and Karim Benzema. Modrić and Kroos. Casemiro and, in the last three years, Vinicius. But mentally that is not easy. Benzema and Zidane were booed by the fans at some point. Even Cristiano, the top scorer in the history of the club. Sometimes you can have incredible talent but at some point the performance drops. But once you leave here it is difficult to reach the same peak of performance. I have seen so many players who gave up and then tried to go somewhere else, but that is difficult.'

Bellingham's first year in Spain was sufficiently impressive to make him a Ballon d'Or contender. Having stated his desire to stay in Madrid for a decade and more he is clearly in it for the long haul. So how much can he achieve? 'He is an example to everyone,' says Ancelotti. 'If he stays here for a long time then he can be captain. And for England he will be.'